CW00457642

In association with Noel Pearson

Defender of
the Faith

By Stuart Carolan

BORD GÁIS
ENERGY SUPPLY

The Abbey Theatre gratefully acknowledges the financial
support from the Arts Council/An Chomhairle Ealaíon

the arts
council
schomhairle
ealaíon

abbeyonehundred

In 2004 the Abbey Theatre celebrates one hundred years as Ireland's national theatre.

Both our programme of on stage work and our programme of ancillary events are particularly exciting and unique to this special year. On stage, the five-season programme has been devised to mark and celebrate the year in a diverse and extensive manner and coheres around five identifiable themes: **The Abbey and Europe; The Abbey and New Writing; Summer at the Abbey; The Abbey and Ireland** and **The Abbey on Tour.** The five key strands to our programme of events comprise **Common Bonds, Facing Forward, "Author, Author", Marking and Remarking** and our **Abbey Birthday** celebration (27th December 2004). These events are in keeping with our philosophy of artistic and social inclusiveness containing a wide range of community, education and artist development programmes.

The Abbey Theatre will present over thirty productions and hundreds of performances in Ireland and throughout the world in 2004 as it reaches out to over a million people.

I hope you enjoy our production of Stuart Carolan's **Defender of the Faith** as part of **The Abbey and New Writing** season.

Welcome to **abbey**onehundred.

Ben Barnes
Artistic Director

Defender of the Faith

By Stuart Carolan

Defender of the Faith by Stuart Carolan was first performed at the Peacock Theatre, Dublin on 16 March 2004. Press night was 22 March 2004.

The play is set in Hackballscross, South Armagh, 1986.

The performance runs without an interval.

Cast in order of appearance

Danny	Shane Murray Corcoran
	Mark McGroarty*
Thomas	Laurence Kinlan
Barney	Tom Hickey
Joe	Gerard McSorley
JJ	Frank McCusker
Man	Lalor Roddy

Director	Wilson Milam
Designer	Dick Bird
Lighting	Paul Keogan
Sound	Cormac Carroll
Fight Director	Donal O'Farrell
Voice Director	Andrea Ainsworth
Stage Director	Audrey Hession
Assistant Stage Manager	Pamela McQueen
Casting Director	Marie Kelly
Set	Abbey Theatre Workshop
Costumes	Abbey Theatre Wardrobe Department
Rehearsal Photographs	Paul McCarthy
Production Photographs	Tom Lawlor
Publicity	Gerry Lundberg PR

Director of the Peacock	Ali Curran

*Member of Anne Kavanagh Young People's Theatre
The Abbey Theatre would like to thank Tom Nyland, Chanelle Veterinar Systems and Eileen O'Neill for their help with this production.

Please note that the text of the play which appears in this volume may be changed during the rehearsal process and appear in a slightly altered form in performance.

Stuart Carolan *Author*

Stuart Carolan was until recently a television and radio producer. This is his first play.

Wilson Milam *Director*

Wilson's Ireland and UK credits include **True West**, Bristol Old Vic, **Flesh Wound**, Royal Court, **The Lieutenant of Inishmore**, RSC, Stratford, Barbican, Garrick, London, **Mr Placebo**, Traverse, Edinburgh, **A Life of the Mind**, Donmar, **The Wexford Trilogy**, Tricycle, **Hurlyburly**, Peter Hall Company at the Old Vic, the Queen's London, **Bug**, Gate Theatre, London, **Killer Joe**, Traverse, Bush, Vaudeville, London. US credits include **Closer**, Berkeley Rep, **Bug**, Wooley Mammouth, Washington DC, **Skeleton**, Shattered Globe, Chicago, **The Caine Mutiny Court Martial**, A Red Orchid, Chicago, **Killer Joe**, Chicago and New York and **A Witness to Temptation** and **American Blues**, Chicago.

Dick Bird *Designer*

Dick's design work includes **The Wind in the Willows**, **The Lady in the Van**, West Yorkshire Playhouse, **Thwaite**, Almeida Theatre, **True West**, **Great Expectations**, Bristol Old Vic, **La Cenerentola**, Opera Theatre Company, **Rabbit**, **Peepshow**, Frantic Assembly Tour, **The Lucky Ones**, Hampstead Theatre, **A Prayer for Owen Meany**, **The Walls**, National Theatre, **Light**, Theatre de Complicite, **Il Tabarro**, **Vollo di Notte**, Long Beach Opera Company, California, **Monkey**, **The Three Musketeers**, Poseidon, **Vagabondage**, The Young Vic, **Closer**, Teatro Broadway, Buenos Aires, **The Invisible College**, Salzberg Festival and **Lucky You**, **Snow Shoes**, Manchester Royal Exchange.

Paul Keogan *Lighting Designer*

Born in Dublin, Paul studied Drama at Trinity College and Glasgow
University. After graduating he worked for the Project Arts Centre as
Production Manager, before leaving to pursue a career as a freelance
lighting designer. His designs for the Abbey and Peacock Theatres
include **Cúirt an Mheán Oíche, The Electrocution of Children, Da** and
The Wild Duck. He designed set and lighting for **The Rite of Spring**
(CoisCéim) and **Chair** (Operating Theatre). Other lighting designs
include **Lady Macbeth of Mtensk** and **The Silver Tassie** (Opera Ireland),
The Lighthouse (OTC), **The Makropulos Case** (Opera Zuid), **Gates of
Gold** and **Performances** (Gate Theatre) and **La Musica** (Siren
Productions).

Cormac Carroll *Sound Designer*

Cormac is from Sligo. His work as a Sound Designer at the Abbey
Theatre includes **Finders Keepers, The House of Bernarda Alba, All my
Sons, The Plough and the Stars, Ariel Da, Eden, Communion, The guys,
For the Pleasure of Seeing Her Again, The Memory of Water, The
Sanctuary Lamp, Made in China, The Morning After Optimism** and
Aristocrats. Other companies worked for include Rough Magic, Bloc One
Theatre, The Hawks Well Theatre and the Gaiety. He recently designed
Shiver at the project for Rough Magic.

Tom Hickey *Barney*

Born Naas, Co Kildare.
"Níl an ceo ag cur isteach air ar chor ar bith"
Old Cavan saying

Laurence Kinlan *Thomas*

Laurence was born in Dublin. His last appearance at the Abbey and Peacock Theatres was in **On Such As We** by Billy Roche. He began his career playing the lead in Alan Bleasdale's drama, **Soft Sand Blue Sea** for Channel 4. He then played Paddy Clohessy in **Angela's Ashes** directed by Alan Parker, **Saltwater** directed by Conor McPherson, **Everlasting Piece** directed by Barry Levinson, **On the Nose**, directed by David Caffrey and **Country** directed by Kevin Liddy. He appeared in **The Bill** directed by David Caffrey and on RTE's **On Home Ground**. Laurence has appeared as one of the leads in Gregor Jordan's **Ned Kelly**, **Veronica Guerin** directed by Joel Schumacher, **Intermission** directed by John Crowley and recently, **The Hard Effect** directed by Lance Daly.

Frank McCusker *JJ*

Frank's first performance at the Abbey was in **The Gentle Island** in 1988. Since then he has appeared in many productions for the company both here and abroad, most recently in Ibsen's **The Wild Duck** at the Peacock. Other theatre work includes performances for the Gate, Druid, Red Kettle, Rough Magic, the RSC and in Harold Pinter's production of **Life Support** with the late Alan Bates in the West End. He has worked extensively in film, television and radio. He has been nominated for an Irish Times/ESB Theatre Award and a Helen Hayes Award in Washington DC.

Gerard McSorley Joe

Gerard McSorley's last appearance at the Abbey Theatre was as Hugh O'Neill in Brian Friel's **Making History**. In recent years he has appeared on the main stage as the Father in **Six Characters in Search of an Author,** Reverend Hale in **The Crucible** and as Michael in the original production of **Dancing at Lughnasa** which transferred to London's National Theatre, the West End and Broadway. He has been making films since 1993, notably, **In the Name of the Father, The Boxer, Michael Collins, Widow's Peak** and **An Awfully Big Adventure**. Recently he appeared as Jack Gilligan in **Veronica Guerin,** Frank Logan in **Bloody Sunday** and has just completed filming **Omagh** for Channel 4 where he played Michael Gallagher.

Lalor Roddy *Man*

Lalor is delighted to be back at the Abbey Theatre. Apart from the Abbey he has worked for the Citizens, the RSC, the Lyric Bickerstaffe, Prime Cut, Tinderbox and the Playhouse.

Our warmest thanks to

Sponsors
Aer Lingus
Anglo Irish Bank
Ferndale Films
Dr. A. J. F. O'Reilly
RTE
Smurfit Ireland Ltd
The Gulbenkian
Foundation
The Irish Times
The Sunday Tribune

Benefactors
AIB Group
An Post
Bank of Ireland
Behaviour and Attitudes
Electricity Supply Board
Guinness Ireland Group
Independent News
and Media, PLC
IIB Bank
Irish Life & Permanent plc
Merc Partners
Pfizer International
Bank Europe
SIPTU
Unilever Ireland Plc

Platinum Patrons
Des Buckley
Lilian & Robert Chambers
Mr. Brian Halford
Donald Helme
Mercer Ltd.
Andrew Parkes
Alan Sheil
Smurfit Corrugated Cases
Total Print and Design
Francis Wintle
Zeus Creative Consultants
Jean Saunders
Bill Shipsey
Avine Lydon

Silver Patrons
Patricia Barnett
Mr. Ron Butler
Joe Byrne
Zita Byrne
Orla Cleary
Ultan Conway
Claire Cronin
Maretti D'Arcy
Cheryl Dickens
Gillian Ennis
Pauline FitzPatrick
Monica Flood
Paul & Florence Flynn
Gerry & Mary Horkan
Irish Actor's Equity
Francis Keenan
Peter Keenan
Gerard Kelly
David Lass
Mary T. Malone
Padraig McCartan
Frank McKeon
Frank & Evelyn Murray

Noeleen Murray
Vincent O'Doherty
John P.H. & Rosemary
O'Reilly
Sumitomo Mitsui
Finance Dublin
Tom Owens
Fr. Frank Stafford
Patricia Thompson
McCullough-Mulvin
Architects

Members
Terence Agnew
Patrick Bannon
Maureen Barron
Dorothy Barry
Kate Bateman
Tony Black
Professor Frank Boland
Ruth Bourke
Caroline Brady
Ms. Jackie Brannigan
Louis Brennan
Francis Britton
Bernard Brogan
Marian & Raymond Burke
Ms. Áine Burke
Eamonn & Anne Cantwell
Ms. Georgina Caraher
Jane Carrigan
Ms. Maureen Carrigan
Elizabeth Carroll
Nicola Clarke
Dr. Brendan Colgan
Eileen Connolly
Margaret Connolly
Michael Connolly
Jim Cooke
Mr. Tom Corcoran
John Corcoran
Brian Corduff
Enda Corneille
Geraldine Corr
Mr. Alan Cox
Ms. Marguerite Cremin
Laura Crowley
Mr. John Cunney
William Cunningham
Ann Curran
Dearbhaill Mahoney
John Delaney
Ms. Tara Delaney
Brigid Doherty
Phelim Donlon
Mr. Pat Donnelly
Cliana Doyle
Eamonn Drea
Cora Dunne
Mr. John Dunne
Judith Elmes
Eleanor Ewings
Mr. Pat Farrell
Michael Finnegan
Mr. Mark Fitzgerald
Jackie Fitzpatrick
Michelle Foley
Enid Gallagher

Josephine Gavigan
Robert P. Gilbert
Anne M. Gilmore
Mr. Michael Glynn
Patrick Goodman
Simon & Carol Gray
Mr. Felimy Greene
Bridie Greene
Leslie Greer
Patricia Halligan
Mr. Bill Harvey
Roger Hatfield
Linda Hawkins
Maeve Heatley
Shay Hennessy
Brian Hickey
Mr. Maurice Hill
Paul Hipwell
Elizabeth Hogan
John Holian
Mary Holian
Ursula Hough Gormley
Mr. Hilary Humphrys
Roger Hussey
Ms. Denise Kane
Kate Kavanagh
Ms. Jane Kealy
Ms. John B. Kelly
Mr. Michael Kennedy
Hilary Kenny
Seamus Killeen
Eve Linders
Paul Linders
Mr. Keith Lowe
Donal & Maire Lowry
Mr. Mark Lynch
Gabrielle Lynch
Francis Lynch
Fechin Maher
Ms. Grainne Macken
Ms. Margaret Mangan
Prof Dermot &
Camilla McAleese
Bernard McCormack
Valerie McCormack
Carmel McCrea
Joseph McCullough
Oonagh McDermot
Mr. Edmund McElligott
Michael & Monica
McGillicuddy
Susan McInerney
Maura McShane
Sandra McCracken
Enda McDonagh
Ms. Ken McDonald
John McGlade
Berna McMenamin
Sean McNicholas
Mr. Ross McParland
Gerard & Mary MacPolin
Gearoid MacUnfraidh
Frank Marshall
Ms. Patricia Mearley
Mr. Alan Moore
Mr. Paul Moran

Ms. Olive Moran
Angela Mulally
Maura & Camillus
Muldowney
Caroline Mullen
John Murphy
Barry Murphy
Mary Murphy
Michael Murphy
Patrick J. Murphy
Robert Murray
Margaret Myron
Mr. Kevin Nealon
Mr. Brendan Nevin
Giuliano Nistri
Ann C. Nolan
Mr. Peter Nolan
Antoinette O'Brien
Beta O'Brian
Seamus O'Cróinín
Tomas O'Cuilinn
Mary O'Donnell
Mary O'Driscoll
Kieran O'Driscoll
Mr. Pol O'Gallichcoir
Mr. Paul O'Grady
Mr. Dermot O'Kelly
Ms. Edel O'Leary
Fionan O'Muircheartaigh
Lucy O'Kelly
Regina & Billy
O'Kelly/O'Shea
Felix O'Regan
Annette & Joe Rowan
Dr. Peter Staunton
Eoghan O'Suilleabhain
Ciaran & Ann O'Sullivan
Terry Patmore
Dr. Collette Pegum
Catherine Power
Heather Quinn
Mr. & Mrs. Reid
Robert Robinson
Mr. Laurence Roe
Patrick. D. Rowan
Beatrice Ryan
Ms. Fiona Scott
Mr. Stratton Sharpe
Ellen Sheerin
Mr. David Sneddon
Mark Sobczyk
Cormac Somers
Margaret Tallon
Mr. John Taylor
Sarah Tully
Martin Vanko
Jennifer Waldron-Lynch
Noreen Walls
Dr. Michael Walsh
Monica Walsh
Richard Walsh
Kevin Warren
Katherine
and Brian
Whidden/Hickey
June Wilkinson
Dr. Jean Whyte

Abbey Theatre

Abbey Theatre Staff

BOARD

Eithne Healy
Chairman

Lorretta Brennan Glucksman
Eugene Downes
Bernard Farrell

John McColgan
Pauline Morrison
Niall O'Brien

John O'Mahony
Michael J. Somers

Artistic Director
Ben Barnes

Managing Director
Brian Jackson

Executive Office
Orla Mulligan

abbeyonehundred
Anne Marie Kane
Sharon Murphy
Jennie Scanlon

Abbey Players
Clive Geraghty
Des Cave

Archive
Mairead Delaney
Aine Kiernan

Assistant Stage Managers
Marella Boschi
Stephen Dempsey
Pamela McQueen

Box Office
Des Byrne
Clare Downey
Adam Lawlor

Box Office Clerks
Catherine Casey
Anne Marie Doyle
Lorraine Hanna
Maureen Robertson
David Windrim

Carpenters
Brian Comiskey
Kenneth Crowe
Mark Joseph Darley
John Kavanagh
Jonathon McDonnell
Kealan Murphy
Bart O'Farrell

Casting
Louise Bracken
Marie Kelly

Cleaning
Joe McNamara

Design
Laura Howe
Maree Kearns

Director of the Peacock
Ali Curran

Finance
Margaret Bradley
Margaret Flynn
Pat O'Connell

Front of House
Pauline Morrison
John Baynes

H.R. Manager
Ciaran McCallion

Honorary Associate Directors
Vincent Dowling
Tomás MacAnna

Information Technology
Dave O'Brien
Ivan Kavanagh

Lighting
Mick Doyle
Brian Fairbrother
Barry Madden
Kevin McFadden

Literary
Jocelyn Clarke
Orla Flanagan
Karin McCully

Maintenance
Michael Loughnane
Tony Delaney

Outreach/Education
Sinead Delaney
Irma Grothuis
Michelle Howe
Jean O'Dwyer

Press & Marketing
Tina Connell
Lynn Dormer
Liz Halpin
Lucy McKeever

Props
Stephen Molloy

Reception
Niamh Douglas
Cheryl Rock
Sandra Williams

Scenic Artists
Angie Benner
Brian Hegarty
Jennifer Moonan

Sound
Eddie Breslin
Cormac Carroll
Nuala Golden

Stage Directors
Finola Eustace
Audrey Hession
John Stapleton

Stage Door
Patrick Gannon
Patrick Whelan

Stage Hands
Aaron Clear
Pat Dillon
Mick Doyle
Des Hegarty
Paul Kelly

Stage Managers
John Andrews
Gerry Doyle

Technical
Vanessa Fitz-Simon
Tommy Nolan
Peter Rose
Tony Wakefield

Ushers
Sarah Buckley
Con Doyle
Neil Gallagher
Barry Gleeson
John Holten
Ronan Keenan
Dolores Murphy
Donna Murphy
Jim O'Keefe

Voice Director
Andrea Ainsworth

Wardrobe
Catherine Fay
Sandra Gibney
Patsy Giles
Vicky Miller
Niamh Lunny
Joan O'Clery
Mandy Scott

**Writer-in-Association
sponsored by
Anglo Irish Bank**
Declan Hughes

Advisory Council
Minister for Arts,
Sport and Tourism
Minister for Finance
Kathleen Barrington
Frank Cuneen
Paddy Duffy
Clare Duignan
John Fairleigh
Clive Geraghty
Des Geraghty
Peadar Lamb
Fergus Linehan
John Lynch
Tomás MacAnna
Patricia McBride
Muriel McCarthy
Jimmy Murphy
Donal Nevin
Edna O'Brien
Ulick O'Connor
Pat O'Reilly
Peter Rose
John Stapleton

DEFENDER OF THE FAITH

Stuart Carolan

For my brother Damien

4

Characters

THOMAS (TOMMY), *twenty*

DANNY, *his brother, ten to twelve*

FATHER (JOE), *late forties*

BARNEY, *works on the farm, fifties*

JJ, *Belfast man, forties*

UNKNOWN MAN

Scene One

1986. Hackballscross, border of Louth / South Armagh. Typical farm kitchen / living room. Table, chairs, armchairs, dresser, telly, a Stanley cooking stove. A scullery with sink on one side and a door on other side leading to bedrooms. Two windows, one with view of South Armagh countryside, other with a view of farmyard sheds. Framed pictures of family, including one picture of brother Shamey in confirmation suit.

Ten-year-old DANNY, *dressed as a pilot with a patch over his left eye, is sitting beneath the kitchen table. He is wearing 'farm goggles'. A bent pitchfork acts as the plane's joystick.* DANNY *makes sound effects of plane going down.*

DANNY. Looks like I'm done for, Tommy. The plane's going down.

DANNY*'s older brother* THOMAS, *twenty, is at the table reading a newspaper. He says nothing.*

Come on, Tommy. Play the game.

THOMAS. I'm reading the paper. What?

DANNY. Play the game, Tommy. Come on. The plane's going down.

THOMAS (*plays along grudgingly*). Was it the black-orange bastard that got you?

DANNY. Tommy, play the game proper!

THOMAS. What do you mean, Danny? Was it not a black-orange bastard that got you? (*Taking the piss.*)

DANNY. No. It's the Red Baron. You know that. Say it.

THOMAS *sighs. Loudly, slowly exaggerating:*

THOMAS. Okay. (*Playing along.*) Was it the Red Baron what got you, Danny?

DANNY. Who else, Tommy? Who else would it be, only the Red Baron himself.

THOMAS (*taking the piss again*). Not some black-orange bastard then?

DANNY. Tommy, you said!

THOMAS. I said what?

DANNY. You said you'd do it right.

THOMAS (*playing along*). How is the plane holding up then, Major Colonel Danny Farquar Upyerholeson?

DANNY. There's bullet holes in her right wing and the tail is destroyed. Come in Tommy? Come in Tommy? Mayday! Mayday!

THOMAS. What about her left wing, Major Danny? How's the left wing holding up?

DANNY. I can't see the left wing Tommy, on account of having only one eye. Got to go now Tommy? She's going to crash. I'll have to bail out. Oh no! Where's me parachute? I don't have me parachute.

THOMAS (*taking the piss again*). Maybe some black-orange bastard robbed it on you.

JOE, *the boys'* FATHER *arrives. He is in his forties, built like a bull, he looks hardy and quick to anger. With him is* BARNEY, *early fifties, an odd-job man about the farm.* BARNEY *has his hat in his hand. He has a slightly deferential air.*

BARNEY. How's the boys?

THOMAS. Well Barney?

BARNEY. Tommy.

FATHER. What's going on? What the fuck are you doing under there, boy?

DANNY. Nothing.

FATHER. You're not doing nothing.

DANNY. I'm not doing anything.

THOMAS. He's not doing anything.

FATHER. What are you doing?

THOMAS. Sure he's only playing. He's pretending to be a pilot.

DANNY. Like Biggles.

FATHER. Biggles? Who the fuck is Biggles? Have you ever heard tell of Biggles, Barney?

BARNEY. I have not, Joe. I wouldn't know who he was. Indeed and I would not.

FATHER. Who the fuck is Biggles?

DANNY. He's a pilot in the war and – (*gulp*) – and he has adventures against the Germans.

FATHER. Against the Germans? Sure the Germans were on our side in the war. Didn't they help Roger Casement with the guns?

DANNY (*doesn't know what to say*). It's from a book . . . He's a pilot in a book.

FATHER. He's a pilot in a book. Have ye ever heard the like, Barney?

BARNEY. I have not, Joe. Indeed I have not.

FATHER. He's a pilot in a book. In the name a Jasus? A fucking Brit pilot. (*Sighs.*) Ah you're the mother's son right enough. He's his mother's son, Barney.

BARNEY. Oh he is surely.

THOMAS. He's only playing. Sure most days he plays at being Francis Hughes. Isn't that right, Danny?

DANNY. That's 'cause when I grow up, I'll be like Francis Hughes. The most wanted man in Ireland.

THOMAS. And what happens if they arrest you, Danny?

DANNY. I'll say up the Provos. Up the rebels. That's what I'll say.

FATHER. That's a good boy, Danny. You don't need to be reading them Brit books. You should be reading about Padraig Pearse? He only had the wan fucking eye as well. Did you know that, Barney?

BARNEY. Oh I heard tell of that right enough.

FATHER. That's why they could only take pictures of him from the side. Did you know that?

BARNEY. Oh so I believe. That's why the man wore glasses. Only the wan eye.

FATHER. He did not wear glasses. In the name a fuckin' cuntin' Jasus, Barney, glasses? Sure why would he wear glasses? Sure what fuckin' use would glasses be to him if the eye didn't work? Answer me that wan, boy! Hi!

BARNEY. Sure I could be wrong, Joe. I don't rightly know.

FATHER. Glasses. In the name a cuntin' Jasus!

BARNEY. I thought his other eye didn't work too well neither, you see, Joe, and . . .

FATHER. There was nothing wrong with his other eye, Barney. It was only the wan eye he had the problem with. Do you get me?

BARNEY. Sure honest to God, Joe, I don't know. I'm not the fella to be asking at all whether it was wan eye or the two eyes that worked. Anyways you'd only need wan eye to wink at a Brit. (*Makes aiming gesture, as if looking through the sight of a rifle.*) Am I right, young man? Hi! Am I right?

BARNEY *winks at* THOMAS.

FATHER. I'm not asking you, Barney. I'm tellin' you. There was nothing wrong with Pearse's other eye, boy.

BARNEY. Sure if you say so, Joe. If you say so.

DANNY. But, hi, Biggles has two eyes.

FATHER (*exasperated*). He has two eyes?

DANNY *nods*.

Then why the fuck do you have a fuckin' patch over wan
of . . . Jasus. I give up. I fuckin' give up . . . (*Exits, shaking
his head.*) . . . Come on, Barney, to fuck and we'll get this
trailer unloaded.

BARNEY. Right so, Joe. See you so, boys.

THOMAS. I'll see you later, Barney.

BARNEY. Indeed and you will. You will surely. Indeed and
you will. (BARNEY *exits*.)

DANNY *gets up from under the table and sits down beside*
THOMAS.

DANNY. But Biggles does too have two eyes.

THOMAS. Danny, will you shut the fuck up and don't be
putting the aul fella in a bad mood. Stick to playing Francis
Hughes to fuck.

DANNY. Sorry Tommy!

THOMAS. Look Danny. Don't be sulkin'. It's not your fault . . .
There's other things the matter with him.

DANNY. Like what?

THOMAS. Nothing.

DANNY. But what?

THOMAS. Nothing, only things.

DANNY. What sort of things?

THOMAS. Things that you needn't be worried about.

DANNY. Will Dad be going to jail again, do you think?

THOMAS. No, Danny. He will not be going to jail again.
Don't worry about it. We'll be fine. Now take that shit off
yer face.

DANNY *pulls the goggles and eyepatch off and leaves them
on the table.*

DANNY. Thomas?

THOMAS *is looking at Shamey's picture on the dresser.*

Thomas, does me Daddy not know that I hate the Brits as much as he does and you do?

THOMAS. Of course he knows, Danny. Of course he knows that.

DANNY. Because I do hate them. The Brit bastards . . . But, but I do like reading about Biggles as well, so I do.

THOMAS. I know, Danny. Sure we all the hate the Brits.

DANNY. I do hate them, so I do.

THOMAS. Sure I know you do. You do surely. Why wouldn't you?

DANNY. I hate them. They're always stopping us on the road and saying hi, Danny Boy, tell your father we'll get him.

THOMAS. Who said this to you?

DANNY. This Brit that stopped us last week. Tell that murderin' Provo father we'll get him, says he.

THOMAS. Harassing childer is all they're good for, Danny.

DANNY. But I'm not a child, Tommy.

THOMAS. Of course you're not.

DANNY. And he says to me, he says, your father, do you know he kills babies and blows up shoppin' centres?

THOMAS. Sure what shoppin' centres are there to blow up around here? Hi! None! That's only fuckin' Brit propaganda, boy. Don't mind that! Fuckin' shopping centres and killin' babies. Dirty Black Brit propaganda from dirty fucking Brit soldiers like, like fuckin' . . . Biggles.

DANNY. Like Biggles?

THOMAS. That's right, like fuckin' Biggles.

DANNY. Well fuck Biggles, I say.

THOMAS. Fuck Biggles is right, Danny.

DANNY. He can go fuck himself, so he can.

THOMAS. He can go fuck himself is right, boy. Give me some peace now till I finish reading the paper, Danny!

DANNY. Alright so . . . You know, Tommy, sometimes they do say things about you and they be trying to ask me questions about you.

THOMAS *continues reading the paper. Pause.*

THOMAS. What kind a questions?

DANNY. Oh, you know, like who's this fella and who's that fella and what's in your bag and we'll get that bastard brother of yours, he's a Provo as well and we'll shoot him and throw him in the river. Or dump him down the cross with a bag over his head. And everybody'll think that it was the Provos that did him. And that he was an informer. They won't do that to you, will they, Tommy?

THOMAS. They won't, Danny. You just ignore them, Danny. They're only trying to get a rise from ye, so they are. That's what they're at. That's all they're good for. Trying to get a rise out of ya, boy.

DANNY. Well they won't get a rise out a me, so they won't, boy.

THOMAS. That's the way, Danny. You tell them nothing.

DANNY. I say to them, I'm not answerin' your questions. You'll have to talk to my solicitor first, so you will.

THOMAS *(laughs)*. You're some boy, Danny, what are you?

DANNY. I'm some boy!

THOMAS. You're some boy right enough.

DANNY. The only thing I'll say to them bastards is nothing except . . . Fuck Biggles.

THOMAS. Fuck Biggles is right enough for them, Danny.

DANNY. Fuck Biggles and fuck the Brits and fuck them all.

FATHER *enters the kitchen. He stares. A volcano about to erupt. He pauses for a few moments before saying anything.*

FATHER. There's a spoon in the yard. A fuckin' spoon in the yard! Will wan of you little cunts get out into that yard and take the fucking spoon back in. Is it too much to ask yese? Is it? I suppose you're getting too big now? Mister Tommy Big fuckin' Shot?

THOMAS *meets his* FATHER*'s stare.* DANNY *looks down.*

I'll ask you again. Who left the spoon out there? Which wan of youse was it? . . . I'm askin' ya a simple fuckin' question. Who left the spoon out there? In the name a Jasus will someone answer me?

THOMAS. I'll get the spoon.

FATHER. I didn't ask you to get the fuckin' spoon. I asked you which wan of youse left the spoon out there. (*Looks at* DANNY.) Danny?

DANNY. It wasn't me.

FATHER. It wasn't you? Sure it had to be somebody.

THOMAS. Leave him to fuck alone. I said already. I'll get the spoon.

FATHER. You stay where you are. Danny, go on out there and get the spoon. And bring that pitchfork back out with you.

DANNY *leaves through the back door.*

I give up. Is it too much to ask yese if you bring a spoon into the backyard to take it back in? Is it?

THOMAS. I didn't take the fucking spoon out.

FATHER *looks at him.*

Why didn't you bring it back in, if you saw it out there?

FATHER. What did ya say?

THOMAS *looks back defiantly.*

THOMAS. I said why didn't you bring the spoon back in. If you saw the spoon out in the yard, why did you leave it out there? We don't know who left the spoon out there. But you fucking come in and start, 'Who left the spoon there?'

'Which one of youse cunts left the spoon there?' I don't
fucking know! Somebody else! What does it matter
anyway? Somebody else left the fucking spoon in the yard.
Not fucking me and not Danny. But if you saw it out there,
why didn't the fuck didn't you bring it in? Or send fucking
Barney in with it?

FATHER. Listen son. I'll tell you this once. When you're
under my fuckin' roof, watch your fuckin' mouth.

THOMAS. Well I'll move out then. 'Cause it's only a fuckin'
spoon.

FATHER. It's not only a spoon. It's wan of your mother's
spoons.

THOMAS. It's a special spoon, then?

FATHER. It's wan of your mother's spoons. And you know
well that your mother liked to keep the place clean. Know
where everything was. Forks and knives and spoons as well.
I'm just trying to do me best for youse . . . With your
mother gone an' all. Do you not believe me?

THOMAS *shrugs*.

Well don't believe me then. It's not my fault.

THOMAS. No, it's never your fault.

FATHER. Well how is it my fault, then?

THOMAS. Well sure that's what I'm after saying, it's never
your fault.

FATHER. How it is my fault? Sure Shamey was the wan
looked up to you. I'm only saying that it couldn't be helped.

THOMAS. What's Shamey got to do with it?

FATHER. I'm just saying don't be going blamin' me for
Shamey.

THOMAS. No, that *was* my fault.

FATHER. I'm not saying that was your fault now. I'm only
saying you could have kept an eye on him.

THOMAS. I'm not my brother's keeper.

FATHER. Oh you're not your brother's keeper is right enough.

THOMAS. You're sayin' it was my fault?

FATHER. All I'm saying is as you yourself said, you weren't your brother's keeper.

THOMAS. Sure you were the one who . . .

DANNY *enters.*

DANNY. I can't find the spoon so I can't. I've looked all over the yard.

FATHER. Well keep fuckin' looking, then. Can't fuckin' find the fuckin' spoon. Sure I'm only after seein' it out there.

THOMAS. I'll come out and help you look for it in a wee while, Danny.

DANNY *exits.* FATHER *looks at* THOMAS. *Pause.*

FATHER. I want you to get Danny to stay with his cousins for a couple of days.

THOMAS. Why?

FATHER. Ah no matter. There's a fella coming down from Belfast is all.

THOMAS (*nods*). Why is that?

FATHER. He's coming down from Belfast so he is.

THOMAS. But why's he coming down?

FATHER. JJ McMahon is his name. Me and him go back a good bit, so we do. JJ's going to be looking into a problem we might be having.

THOMAS. What problem?

FATHER. A problem with security.

THOMAS. Is there just him?

FATHER. There's just him.

THOMAS. Why no-one else?

FATHER. Listen, I need to sort this thing out sooner rather than later otherwise the Boss man will sort it out himself and he'd go at it like a bull.

THOMAS. The Boss man's not going to be too happy when he finds out you've brought an outsider in.

FATHER. Don't you worry about the Boss man. I'll worry about him. The Boss man might be a thick cunt but he's not stupid. He'll be all right.

THOMAS. Who do you think it is?

FATHER. It could be anybody. It could be nobody. Don't say –

DANNY. Hi, I looked everywhere so I did. I couldn't find it.

He's ignored.

FATHER. – a fuckin' word.

THOMAS. Sure what would I say?

FATHER. Fuck all is what you'll say.

DANNY. Daddy, I looked everywhere but I couldn't find it.

FATHER. What couldn't you fuckin' find?

Fade to black.

Scene Two

The next day. Early evening. Farmhouse kitchen again.
FATHER *and* THOMAS *have had their tea.* THOMAS *is making a hot drop.*

THOMAS. Your pal JJ has soft hands.

FATHER. What?

THOMAS. I said his hands are soft. Soft hands.

FATHER. In the name a Jasus, what are you shitein' on about. 'He's got soft hands.'

THOMAS. All I'm saying is the man has soft hands.

He pours himself a tea. Looks in the milk jug. Goes to the fridge in the scullery.

FATHER. Jesus Christ, there might be a tout in the house and you're talking about his hands. Will ye get the fuck away with your fuckin' soft fuckin' hands?

THOMAS. Fuck it. I won't open my mouth so. (*Looking in the fridge.*) We're out of milk.

FATHER. Listen son, they say you can judge a man by his shoes. They're wrong. You know why? A man can wear an old pair of shoes with holes in them and what does that tell you about him?

THOMAS *shrugs.*

THOMAS. We're out of milk.

FATHER. Fuck the milk. What does it tell you about him?

THOMAS. That's he can't afford a new pair of shoes?

FATHER (*disgusted, shaking his head*). No, it fuck . . . (*Sighs and shakes his head again.*) No, it tells you fuck all. It tells you nothing about him. Not wan thing.

THOMAS. Jasus, and there I was thinking the Boss man was paranoid. All I said was the man had soft little hands. That's it.

FATHER. Leave the Boss man out of this. What I'm trying to say to you, son, is don't judge a man on whether he has soft hands or not. Ye can no more judge a man by how soft his hands is than . . .

FATHER *sees JJ as he enters from the hallway.*

JJ *has known the FATHER, JOE, for some years. There is an easy way between the two of them that only comes with time. JJ is charming, honest and amicable. He has an open face, his appearance and clothes are nondescript. He is without affectation. However, he is also possessed of a forensic intelligence that differs from JOE's animal cunning.*

Well JJ.

JJ. All right, Joe?

FATHER. Did you have a good rest?

JJ (*yawning*). I had a nice wee kip there. Slept like a baby.
Woke up every half-hour looking for me mammy's tit. How
are you, son?

FATHER. This fella's the eldest. Thomas. Sure you met before.
Named after Thomas Aquinas. Are you hungry?

JJ. No thanks, Joe. I'm all right. I'm grand. But I'd take a wee
drop a tea in my hand. That'd do me, Joe.

FATHER. We're out of milk for the tae, JJ.

JJ. Doesn't matter, Joe. Doesn't matter. Black will do rightly.
So you're Tommy?

THOMAS *nods.*

Well, Tommy, come here to me; don't mind what yarns this
fella's been telling you about me. Right? All of it is lies.

FATHER. His mother named him so she did.

THOMAS. Of course me mother named me. And you named
me. Sure who else would have named me if not me mother
and father?

JJ. You're named after Saint Thomas Aquinas?

FATHER. Named after Thomas Aquinas is right. Aye, it was a
hard birth for the mother like. The young fella didn't seem
to want to get born at all, did ya hi!

THOMAS. Fuck off.

FATHER. And says she to a nun there in the hospital, what date
is it? And says the nun, it's the third of July, missus. What
Saint has that day says the mother? Today is the feast day
of Saint Thomas Aquinas says the nun and says the mother
back, well in that case I'll say a prayer to Thomas Aquinas
so I will and if he helps me through this and it's a boy, I'll
name him Thomas Aquinas.

JJ. But the third of July, that's the feast day of Saint Thomas
More, Joe. Thomas Aquinas is January 28th.

THOMAS. Away to fuck!

FATHER. That can't be. Sure the nun in the hospital said it to the mother.

THOMAS. Fuck! How come you know something like that? Not even a priest would know that.

JJ. I have a head for useless information is all that is, Tommy. That and two years trainin' to be a priest.

FATHER. That's right. I forgot that. JJ used to say it was a choice between holy orders and last orders. (*Laughs.*)

JJ. If it had a bin Bacardi and Coke instead of fuckin' altar wine in the chalice I might a stayed, Joe! (*Laughs.*)

THOMAS. Who was Saint Thomas More then?

JJ. He was a Sir before he became a Saint. Advisor to Henry VIII is what he was.

FATHER. That's the fella that chopped the heads off his wives.

THOMAS. No, that was a different Henry VIII.

FATHER. You shut your fuckin' hole. But JJ, I thought he was a Prod?

JJ. Aye, he was. But he was born a Catholic. The Pope gave Henry the title 'Defender of the Faith' he did such a good job defending Catholic rights, but it was really Sir Thomas More who deserved the title.

FATHER. And tell me this JJ, what did the man do?

THOMAS. He chopped off his wives' heads. Are you not listenin'?

FATHER. I fuckin' know that. Watch your fucking manners. I'm askin' JJ.

THOMAS. Why the fuck do you care?

FATHER. What the fuck are you at? I'm asking the man a fucking simple enough question. Let JJ tell the story. Sorry JJ, go on, you were sayin'.

JJ. Well to cut a long story short, Henry VIII wanted to divorce his wife and the Pope wouldn't let him, so Henry decides to set up his own church and become a Protestant. So in other words, he takes the soup. And Thomas More wouldn't go along with it, so the head was taken off him and he became a saint.

Pause.

FATHER. Jasus, I can't believe the mother got that wrong.

JJ. What's that, Joe?

FATHER. I'm only sayin', JJ, that I can't believe the mother got it wrong on the names.

THOMAS. Sure didn't the nun give her the wrong information? What does it matter?

FATHER. I know but she could a checked.

THOMAS. How could she a checked?

FATHER. She could a asked a priest. That would be what I would call checking now.

THOMAS. Sure she did check. She checked with a nun. The nun got it wrong.

FATHER. I'm only saying she could a done a proper job checking the facts.

THOMAS. How was Mammy to know the nun would get it wrong?

FATHER. I'm not blaming your mother. Sure what fucking matter how you got your name. What do you think I'll be away off to the nuthouse to see your Mammy and says I, Mammy you've named Thomas after the wrong saint. I'm sorry but I'll have to chop your fucking head off. (*Laughing.*)

THOMAS. It's not a nuthouse, it's a hospital.

FATHER. It's a hospital for nutters. You have to face facts, Thomas. What else would you call a hospital for nutters only a nuthouse?

THOMAS. You're some cunt, so you are.

FATHER. Thomas, there's no point pretending she's at a holiday camp for the weekend. It's a nuthouse. There's no other word for it.

THOMAS. Fuck off. I'll see you later, JJ. Maybe I might visit Mammy in the nuthouse. I could pretend I'm her husband up for a visit.

FATHER. Stop now, Thomas.

THOMAS. It'd make a nice change anyway, her husband up for a visit but sure the shock might kill her. (THOMAS *makes to go.*)

FATHER. Thomas, sit down to fuck and talk to JJ. And stop acting like a cunt. I have to go out. JJ, will you be all right? (*Goes into the scullery to get his coat.*)

JJ. Don't mind me, Joe. I'm the least of your problems.

THOMAS. Where are you off to?

FATHER. Don't you worry about me or where I'm going. You sit there and look after JJ. I'll talk to you later, JJ. I'm just going down to the shop now. I'll have the milk for your tae when I come back.

JJ. No problem, Joe. You do what you have to do.

FATHER *exits.* THOMAS *sits down. Silence.*

Do you mind if I ask you a question, Tommy?

THOMAS *looks at him.*

Why does your father need to go out and get milk?

THOMAS. Sorry. I don't get you.

JJ. Why does he need to buy a pint of milk from the shop?

THOMAS. Well because we're out of milk, JJ, would be the simple answer.

JJ. But why go to the shop when you milk cows? Do you see what I mean?

THOMAS. I see what you mean.

JJ. So why go to the shop for the milk?

THOMAS. It tastes nicer from the shop, so it does.

JJ nods. Silence.

JJ. Soft hands, Tommy. Seemingly I have soft hands.

THOMAS looks up.

THOMAS. Well as long as it's only your hands that are soft, JJ.

JJ. But never judge a man on whether he has soft hands or not. Am I right?

THOMAS. I suppose.

JJ. Well that's what your father always says, Tommy. Never judge a man on whether he has soft hands, shiny shoes or goes to the shop to get a pint of milk when he has gallons of it in his shed. Am I right?

THOMAS looks at him, irritated.

Don't worry, Tommy. I'm only havin' the craic. All I got was the arse end of what you were saying. (*Begins to examine his hands.*)

THOMAS. Sorry. I didn't mean . . .

JJ. Well it's true. (*Mimics.*) Mammy, Mammy, why are you're hands so – (*Sings.*) – soft hands from Fairy Liquid. (*Laughs.*)

THOMAS smiles.

THOMAS. We have a diseased cow. That's why we're not using our own milk. She's got an infection. We milk her separately and throw away her milk, and send the rest of the milk to the creamery as usual.

JJ. So you can't use the rest of the milk.

THOMAS. Well we could. But you don't want to take a chance with gettin' sick for a couple of days around here. So that's why it's better to use the milk from the shop. That's all there is to it.

JJ keeps looking at him.

Why?

JJ. No why. I was only asking. (*Looks at his hands.*) Soft hands.

THOMAS. Well what do they say? Soft hands, hard heart.

JJ. No, that's cold hands, warm heart.

THOMAS. Same difference I suppose. What would you be, JJ, hard man, cold heart?

JJ. No, I'm not a hard man, Tommy. The day you think you're a hard man is the day you're done for in this game. It's like the oak tree and the blade of grass in the storm, oak tree gets uprooted, storm doesn't knock a stir out o' the blade of grass.

THOMAS. And that's the way you are?

JJ. That's the way we all should be, Tommy.

THOMAS. So you don't think you're a hard man?

JJ. I'm not a hard man. I'm a soldier. It's that simple. I have no romantic illusions about militarism.

THOMAS. What the fuck does that mean?

JJ. It means sometimes you have to harden your heart is all. And you become . . . hardened isn't the right word. Inured. You become inured.

THOMAS. Inured?

JJ. Inured.

Silence.

Shop milk.

THOMAS. What's that?

JJ. A nice pint of shop milk.

THOMAS. What?

JJ. A pint of milk from the shop. Isn't that what it is? A pint of shop milk. Milked from a silky cow by the softest of soft hands.

Fade to black.

Scene Three

The next day. A five-bar gate in the yard. The sound of helicopters overhead and barking dogs.

BARNEY (*looking up*). Bastards.

FATHER. Fucking cunts.

BARNEY. Cunts is right.

FATHER. Did you take a look at that sick cow today?

BARNEY. I did surely when I did the milkin' this morning, Joe.

FATHER. Well you need to be checkin' on her again soon enough. The noise of them fuckin' things sends the dogs mad, so it does. (*Calls out to dogs.*) Shut up to fuck, hi.

BARNEY. The dogs is great all the same, havin' them around the place.

FATHER. Not when they've bin driven demented with the Brit helicopters all the time. (*Calls out again.*) Shut up to fuck will youse, hi. Thomas! Thomas! Where the fuck is he?

BARNEY. Sure they have to have something to bark about.

FATHER. What?

BARNEY. The dogs. I was sayin' they have to have something to bark about.

FATHER. It's worse for the fucking cattle. That's what gives the cows them heart attacks. Did you know that Barney? The noise from the helicopters.

BARNEY. Cows get heart attacks?

FATHER. They do surely. Sure two of them dropped dead on us in the space of the last year alone, boy.

BARNEY. That was from heart attacks?

FATHER. Aye, from heart attacks. Sure why else would a cow drop stone-dead like that? For no good reason.

BARNEY. I thought it would be old age.

FATHER. Old age? For fuck's sake, Barney. Old fucking age! No, they get frikened be the noise and it sends their hearts all a flutter.

BARNEY. Why does it only happen to wan or two then and not the others, Joe?

FATHER. Sure how would I know, Barney? Do I look like a fuckin' vet, boy?

Silence for a moment.

BARNEY. I suppose ye find that in all walks of life. There's some that can take it and there's others that can't.

FATHER. You do surely . . . (FATHER *looks round. Pause.*) Where's that fucking cunt now? Thomas! Thomas! Get out here to fuck and shut those fucking dogs up.

BARNEY. The dogs don't get heart attacks all the same.

FATHER. Not that I heard tell of. The Brits hate the dogs, so they do. Did you know that, Barney? The Englishman's best friend? And haven't they poisoned at least five of ours in the last few years.

BARNEY. Some best friend, boy. A nice way to treat your best friend like that, going around poisoning him.

FATHER. The dogs hate the Brits just as much as the Brits hate the dogs.

BARNEY. Sure if someone was going around trying to poison you, you'd hate them fairly soon, right enough. Or you'd have difficulties trustin' them anyway. You would surely . . . Why do you think the Brits hate the dogs, Joe?

FATHER. I think, Barney, they hate the dogs on account of the dogs can sniff them out.

Dogs have stopped barking.

Dogs can sniff out a Brit observation post for half a mile. (*Smells the air.*)

BARNEY. Is that a fact? It's no wonder then, they do hate them.

FATHER. Sure the cows can do the same. If there's something amiss in a field, they'll all be sniffing around the wan spot.

BARNEY. Like sheep.

FATHER (*looks at* BARNEY. *Pause*). No, like cows, Barney. Like fuckin' cows . . . (*Pause.*) . . . Sure there's fuck all places for Brits to hide around here even when they want to.

BARNEY. And sure God knows they want to.

FATHER. It's fuck all use their SAS training is around here. They can stay in the wan hole in the ground, not move, have their breakfast, dinner and tae in the hole and shite into a bag and makes not wan bit of difference if you have the cattle sniffin' around.

BARNEY (*pause*). Or dogs.

FATHER (*looks at him bemused*). Or dogs is right, Barney. (*Spots* THOMAS *in the distance.*) Ah here he is now.

BARNEY. True enough. True enough . . . Yonder collie seems very big about the belly, so she does.

FATHER. Ah she is surely. Any day now and she'll be having the pups, boy.

BARNEY. They won't last too long around here, hi.

FATHER. They will not. (THOMAS *enters.*) Where were you, bolloxey?

THOMAS. Nowhere.

FATHER. Nowhere. Where's nowhere? Have you ever heard tell of a place called nowhere, Barney?

BARNEY. No, Joe. I have not.

FATHER. Fucking nowhere. Will you go down and sort out them dogs and stop them fucking howling?

THOMAS. Sure they've stopped.

FATHER. They've stopped? Do you hear that, Barney? They've stopped?

BARNEY. Well in fairness, Joe, they have stopped.

FATHER. They've stopped. I've fuckin' . . . Jesus Christ . . .
I fuckin' don't know.

THOMAS. JJ wants to see you up at the house.

FATHER. He wants to see me?

THOMAS. Aye, up at the house.

FATHER. He wants to see me up at my own house?

THOMAS. That's what I said.

FATHER. I know that's what you said. He wants to see me up
at my own fuckin' house. Who the fuck does he think he is?

THOMAS. Well you're the fucking one who sent for him.

FATHER *looks at him.* THOMAS *shouldn't have said that.*

FATHER. You shut your fuckin' mouth. Barney, I want you to
take another look at that sick cow. Will you do that?

BARNEY. I will surely, Joe. I will surely.

FATHER *exits.*

THOMAS. Fucking cunt!

BARNEY. Fucking cunt is right!

THOMAS *laughs.*

Well he can be betimes. He can be a right cunt.

THOMAS. Betimes?

BARNEY. Ah he's not the worst.

THOMAS. Going on about the fucking dogs. I'd say Bobby
will pop her pups before the day is out.

BARNEY. Tommy, don't now!

THOMAS. Don't what? What, Barney?

BARNEY. You know yourself, Tommy.

THOMAS. I know what?

BARNEY. You know that dog's name is Spot.

THOMAS. But how can she be called Spot when she doesn't have any spots? She's a fuckin' collie.

BARNEY. You know what I'm talking about. Your father would hit the roof.

THOMAS. Barney, what the fuck is wrong with namin' her after Bobby Sands. The man was a fucking hero.

BARNEY. He was a hero is right and you can't be namin' dogs after him. Streets in Libya is wan thing but not dogs.

THOMAS. It's Tehran, Barney.

BARNEY. What's that?

THOMAS. Tehran. That's where they have the street named after him. That's in Iran, not Libya.

BARNEY. It doesn't matter a fuck where it is. Naming a dog after a dead hunger striker is not right. Anyway sure Bobby's a boy's name.

THOMAS. Not in America.

BARNEY. Will you go away to fuck now, Tommy, and don't be annoyin' me.

THOMAS. Barney. I'm only havin' ya on.

BARNEY. Well you can't be jokin' about things like that. Whatever way you look at it, it won't make wan bit of difference to the pups.

THOMAS. I suppose not.

BARNEY. It will not. Sure it's the same every year. The little Jack Russell gets up on her – I don't know how he does it but he does – and then three, four months later and your father is drownding them down in that barrel of water at the back of the house.

Silence. Talk of the pups has made THOMAS *wistful.*

Your father's not a bad man, Tommy. He's just the way he is.

THOMAS. Listen Barney. I'm not a fucking child. I'm not looking for him to wipe my arse and tuck me up in bed at night and read me bedtime stories.

BARNEY. You had your mother for that.

THOMAS. I did. She did read us bedtime stories. You know that, Barney?

BARNEY. I didn't know that.

THOMAS. We had to be in bed before she would tell them. Me and Shamey. Homework done. Teeth brushed and then she'd come in and sit down on the floor between the two beds. 'Once upon a time,' she'd always begin.

BARNEY. Once upon a time there were two little boys.

THOMAS. Aye. Two little boys. One called Tommy and the other called Shamey.

BARNEY. And what would they do?

THOMAS. Have adventures. I can't remember now. (*He is thinking.*) I was up at the hospital a few weeks ago and I asked her about them and you know what she said?

BARNEY. What did she say?

THOMAS. She said the stories were wrong. (*Starts to get upset.*)

BARNEY. Wrong, Tommy?

THOMAS. She said they didn't make any sense. They were all wrong.

BARNEY. Jasus, Tommy, sure they were only stories for childer.

THOMAS. I know but she said they were wrong.

BARNEY. Tommy, come here to me now. They were only stories. Who's to say what's right or wrong only God? Am I right?

THOMAS *nods.*

Of course I'm right. I am surely.

A brief silence.

How is she now? The mother!

THOMAS *shrugs.*

THOMAS. Ah sure . . . It'd be a lot easier if it wasn't for that cunt.

BARNEY. Well he has a lot to be worried about.

THOMAS. He's a cunt.

BARNEY. Ah you can't say that about your father. You boys is all he lives for. I remember the man was lifted, when was it, a good while ago, Easter two years back.

THOMAS. The old man?

BARNEY. Aye . . . it was the Friday after the Easter Monday.

THOMAS. I don't remember that.

BARNEY. Sure why would you? Sure, be rights, the man should be in the *Guinness Book of Records* for the number a times he's been lifted.

THOMAS. And what was so fucking special this time?

BARNEY. Nothing. I'm tryin' to tell. Look it. The point I'm trying to make has nothing to do with him getting lifted.

THOMAS. Well you're talking about it long enough.

BARNEY. Tommy, it's neither here nor there. It's how I remember it. It's what he said about you boys. The point is –

THOMAS. And where was I?

BARNEY. For fuck's sake, Thomas. You were away. Anyway he came back from bein' lifted and says he to me, Barney, keep an eye on them boys if anything ever happens to me.

THOMAS. What like make sure the cows is milked and the bullocks are counted?

BARNEY. No. You know what he meant. He wouldn't have said that now if there wasn't some concern for youser welfare. Keep an eye on them boys is what he said.

THOMAS. And where was Shamey?

BARNEY. I don't rightly remember where he was. Sure you know yourself your father was always getting lifted. It was only for 24 hours I think. You know your father. Would have

sat staring at the wall the whole time. Sayin' nothing only
lookin' at the wall. Always used to say to me, he'd say,
remember, Barney, don't say nothing. If they offer you a
cup a tae or a smoke or how's the weather, say nothing, just
think of something else, pick a spot on the wall and smile to
yourself. Always smile to yourself, he says. The cunts hate
that. They can never figure you out then. They have locked
you up, no sleep, beating the shite out of you, grabbin' your
balls, tellin' you what they'll do to your family, and you
there with a big smile on your face, staring at the wall. Oh
he's a hard man is your father.

THOMAS. I suppose. That's one thing they can't threaten you
with, Barney, your family. We'll kill all your family says
one of them. Sure what family says you? Kill away.

BARNEY. The mother an' father is long dead right enough.

THOMAS. I know, Barney. Sorry, Barney. I didn't mean –

BARNEY. No offence taken, young man. None taken . . .
(*Thinks.*) But I do have a second cousin in Clones, so I do.
She does invite me for the dinner once every so often. I do
have the dinner there then, so I do.

THOMAS. I didn't know that now, Barney.

BARNEY. Well, there ye are now.

THOMAS (*thinking*). Do you mind me asking, Barney, what
do you think of when you get lifted?

BARNEY. What?

THOMAS. I was just wonderin'? You know, what do you think
of to stop them getting into your mind?

BARNEY. Ah just tings I suppose. Starin' at the wall and
saying fuck all. It's hard to say.

THOMAS. But you must be thinking of something?

BARNEY. I do go into a world of me own, so I do. The cunts
would be screamin' and shoutin' and bangin' the table and
sometimes bangin' your head agin the table and I'd be off in
another world like.

THOMAS. But what things would you be thinking of?

BARNEY *looks away.*

Ah go on, Barney, tell me.

BARNEY. Well the last time I was lifted, I was thinking about that fella from Dungannon that was shot in the head and left the other side of the cross.

THOMAS. The informer?

BARNEY. Aye.

THOMAS. Is that not an odd thing to be thinkin' about?

BARNEY. Do you want to hear the story or not?

THOMAS. Sorry! Go on! What about him?

BARNEY. Well I was thinking. What's this his name was?

THOMAS. It doesn't matter.

BARNEY. Jasus, I can't remember. The fella from Dungannon.

THOMAS. Sure it doesn't matter. Mister Fuckin' Tout, Barney.

BARNEY. Well I was thinking, I know the man got what was coming to him.

THOMAS. A fucking good-for-nothing Judas tout bastard. He did surely, boy.

BARNEY. I know that.

THOMAS. And he fuckin' cost lives, boy!

BARNEY. I'm not sayin' –

THOMAS. He was a fucking tout, Barney.

BARNEY. I'm not sayin' he wasn't. Will you fuckin' take it easy, Tommy? You asked me the fuckin' question. I'm only answerin' you. I know the man was a tout. I couldn't give a fuck. I'm only tellin' you.

THOMAS. Sorry, Barney. Go on.

BARNEY. I'm not saying he didn't get what was comin' to him. He did and more than likely it was deserved. It was only that, it was only that I was thinking it was horrid sad, him there, the great big lump of a man that he was, dead on the side of a wet road with no shoes or socks.

THOMAS. Sure what does it matter, no shoes or socks?

BARNEY. Nothing. It doesn't make wan bit a difference as the fella said. It was just. It was raining.

THOMAS. And you thought he might catch his death of cold?

BARNEY. No, I did not. I was only thinking like they could have left the poor man with his shoes and socks. There was something not dacent about that. Him there stone-cold dead on the side of the wet road and the white feet all swollen like a diseased carcass.

THOMAS. Jesus Christ, Barney, are you goin' soft in the head?

BARNEY. I am not. I am not soft in the head so I'm not. I'm not soft in the head at all.

THOMAS. No, you're not, Barney. I don't know what's wrong with me. I'm sorry. I just feel sometimes . . . I don't know.

BARNEY. It's all right, Tommy.

THOMAS. And this fuckin' JJ fella from Belfast. I don't know. I don't know what's worse, havin' a tout or havin' a tout hunt.

BARNEY. And that's why he's here?

THOMAS. Aye, I'm not supposed to say.

BARNEY. Fuckin' hell!

THOMAS. Who do you think it is?

BARNEY. I don't know. But it's very fuckin' peculiar.

THOMAS. How's that?

BARNEY. Well the normal procedure is you mark your man and he's in boot of the car before he knew what hit him. You don't give the fucker a chance to fuck off.

THOMAS. So why don't they do that if they know who it is?

BARNEY. They must not know.

THOMAS. It might only be the Boss man getting fuckin' paranoid.

BARNEY. That wouldn't be a first.

THOMAS. Fuck no. So what about this fucker that you were thinking about?

BARNEY. Ah sure fuck him. That's all I was thinkin' about and sure it was good enough for him.

THOMAS. It was and sure what use would a fella have for shoes or socks if the man's dead? He'd have no use for anything at all.

BARNEY (*trying to lighten the mood*). No, he would not except a wooden box. A fella would need that so he would if he found himself in that predicament. An' a hole in the ground, he'd need that too.

THOMAS. He would.

BARNEY. Oh he would surely . . . (*Thinking.*) Did you know that you have to pay for a grave? I found that the other day. I thought ye'd get them for free. Or the Church would pay for them.

THOMAS. I know that all right, Barney.

BARNEY. Oh so you do, so you do right enough. So you do.

THOMAS. I do. I know that much.

A beat.

BARNEY. Do you be thinkin' about him much, Tommy?

THOMAS. All the time, Barney. All the time. I think about him all the time. Every day. Sure it's only been a year. There was only a year and a half between us, Barney. Fourteen months.

BARNEY. I know that.

THOMAS. But I thought of him I suppose like a child.

BARNEY. Sure he *was* only a child. Indeed that's all he was. Only a child. Not yet a young man.

THOMAS. I know. The worst thing is I can look at the him in the picture but I can't picture him in my head . . . And sometimes I have dreams where I see him getting shot in the dreams or somebody tellin' me he's dead. Coming up to the back door of the house and saying your brother Shamey's been shot. And I'm going sweet God no, please no, no, please God, let him be okay. You can get shot and survive. He'll be all right. He's not dead. And the person's saying, it's too late, Shamey's dead. He's dead. And I'm saying no, no way, this is my worst nightmare, Shamey's dead and then just like that, Shamey walks in the door and says what's all the fuss about boy and I'm thinking thank you God, thank you God, Shamey's all right. He's not dead. And then I'm happy like I've never been happy and then, and then, then I wake up. And for the first couple of minutes I'm happy. I'm still half-asleep and I'm thinking Jasus, that was some nightmare that was. Shamey dead. Jasus. I must tell Shamey I had this nightmare where I thought he was dead.

BARNEY *looks at him with great feeling.*

And then I wake up proper and I remember he *is* dead. He's cold and he's in the ground. Shamey is dead and I can't go and tell him about my dream. Shamey is dead.

BARNEY. But Shamey didn't get shot. He drownded himself.

THOMAS. I know he didn't get shot Barney, but in this dream he does get shot. Not drownded like a fucking pup in a black plastic bag.

Fade to black.

Scene Four

FATHER *and* JJ *are at the kitchen table.* JJ *in silence, looking, sitting.* FATHER *has his face in his hands and sighs as he looks up.*

JJ *is drumming with his fingers.*

JJ. So what do you think, Joe?

FATHER. I don't know.

JJ. So tell me again.

FATHER. So the radio remote control doesn't go off. The boys are pushing the buttons only there's nothing happening.

JJ. Loose wire?

FATHER. No loose wire.

JJ. Battery pack?

FATHER. Should have been in it.

JJ. Was it?

FATHER. Aye, it was. Last time I looked it was. Unless some fucking cunt took it fucking out. The whole lot of us get picked up the next day, all held for seven days, bar wan. And you know who that was?

JJ. You.

FATHER. Aye. They're not stupid. They are not. They let me out after 48 hours. Kept everybody else in for the full whack. I'm there thinking, this is fucking odd. And I could tell as well by the way they were asking me questions, they weren't looking for answers. Aye, that's when I knew we had a problem. The fuckers are trying to finger me.

JJ. Were you talking to the Boss man after you got out?

FATHER. I was. I went over to his place directly. He did the debriefin' himself.

JJ. What did he say?

FATHER. Sure he knew right well what they were at. Says he, them Brits must think I'm a stupid fucking cunt, Joe, says he. They let you out after 48 hours, which is more or less saying, here boys, this man is the informer.

JJ. So what then?

FATHER. Well then we figured, there were two possibilities. Wan, it's only the Brits creating mischief which you have to consider could be a possibility or two, they put the finger on me to cover up for somebody else.

JJ (*taking the piss*). What about number three? Right? You'll like this one, Joe. This is a good one. You're the fucking tout and they only kept you in for the 48 hours to keep up appearances. How do you like that?

FATHER (*going with the wind-up*). You know you're right, JJ. It is me. It's a relief at long last to get it off me chest. How could I have lived with myself for so long?

JJ. Let's look at number two. The bomb doesn't go off, they let you out, keep the others in, why?

FATHER. That's it exactly. Why? Bomb doesn't go off, I'm let out, finger is put on me, boys put two and two together and get fucking fifty-nine.

JJ. Maybe it was a fault with the wiring. These things happen.

FATHER. No, it's not that. I'm fairly sure it's not that.

JJ. But maybe it is. The bomb doesn't go off, Brits see their chance and they start with the head games. Back to number one.

FATHER. No, I don't think so. It doesn't smell right.

JJ. No, it doesn't. So why wait around? You've had three weeks. You know who it is. Get a couple of the boys, bring him across the border and watch him fucking sweat. He'd be crying like a fucking babby in no time.

FATHER. Because I was thinking it might not be Barney. So we question Barney, the other cunt gets wind of this and skips. We're none the wiser. We stiff Barney and the other cunt takes a chance and stays where he is. And it's worse off we are.

Long pause. JJ *is thinking.*

JJ. I'll need to see the Boss man about this.

FATHER. Why's that?

JJ. I have to let him know what I think. You don't think I could be stompin' around here and him not knowing about it.

FATHER. But he okayed it with me and sure I sent the
message to you. Sure it was my idea to bring you in.

JJ. Maybe so, Joe. Maybe so. But sure I had him on to me as
well.

FATHER. Did you?

JJ. I did. Did you not know that?

The banter between the two has started again. FATHER
says nothing.

JJ *(taking the piss)*. He mustn't trust you so.

FATHER. He mustn't is right.

JJ. Would he have any cause not to?

FATHER. Would you go way to fuck, JJ. Sure you know what
the man's like. The man wouldn't trust his own mother. And
you're not without blame in the matter, either ya cunt ya.

JJ. How's it my fault?

FATHER. Sure you're the wan gave him Chairman Mao's
Little Red Book. He wouldn't stop shiteing on about it for
months. Talking about revolutionary fish and fucking
running dogs. It was your fault so it was. Givin' him that
fuckin' cuntin' book.

JJ. But sure, Joe, the fucker could have written the book
himself. He had no need for it.

FATHER. Well he's given up on it now, so he has. Says it's
a load of bollocks that fucking communism. Sure it is too.
Says he, Joe, says he, in my book a communist is someone
with fuck all who wants to share it with everybody. That's
a good wan. But not exactly fuckin' original. Says he, Joe,
all I am is a fucking pig farmer.

JJ. And he does seem to like the pigs right enough.

FATHER. For a fucking pig farmer.

JJ. Pigs are intelligent animals all the same.

FATHER. Like dogs.

JJ. No. They're smarter than dogs. Winston Churchill said he liked the pig himself. Said a cat looks down his nose at us, a dog looks up to us but the pig treats us as equals.

FATHER. Winston Churchill said that? Jasus, that's a good wan. But if pigs were that smart, why could they not stage a mass break-out? Get fuckin' organised.

JJ. They're smart but not that smart.

FATHER. They're fucking dumb beasts is what they are. Otherwise they'd be driving around in top-of-the-range motors an' living in mansions. Or at the very least, you'd have pigs riding around on bikes like dogs in the circus. Or what are the fellas that can juggle balls and they go – (*Gestures.*) – ar, ar, ar. They've got flippers. Like penguins.

JJ (*laughing*). Seals.

FATHER (*laughing*). Them's the boys. They're be a lot smarter than pigs I'd say meself. I've never seen a pig cyclin' around on a bike, or jugglin' balls like them other fellas.

JJ. No, pigs are smart: smarter than dogs or seals. They have the same intelligence as a four-year-old child. Cattle and sheep are dumb beasts but sending a pig to the slaughter-house is like sending a four-year-old child.

FATHER. I suppose that's why they do be squealin' when they're for the chop. They know it's comin'.

THOMAS *enters the scullery. He sits down and begins to take his boots off. He can hear the conversation of his* FATHER *and* JJ.

JJ. I think all animals know it's coming. That's why they try and run.

A beat.

FATHER. They all know when it's comin' right enough.

A beat.

So . . .

JJ. So?

FATHER. So.

JJ. So what do you think?

FATHER. So talking of animals with the brains of a four-year-old . . . I think it's Barney.

JJ *nods.*

I don't like admitting it to myself, JJ, 'cause the fella's been with me going on twenty year. And I feel sorry for sayin' this 'cause poor Barney was dropped on his head a babby would be a nice way of puttin' it. But I think –

THOMAS *enters the kitchen.*

THOMAS. You think what?

FATHER. It's none of your business. Now get the fuck outa here. Me and JJ are havin' a meeting.

THOMAS. You're sayin' Barney's a tout?

FATHER. I didn't say that. I said I *think* Barney might be a tout. There's a big difference.

THOMAS. This is crazy. There's no way Barney is an informer.

FATHER. You shut the fuck up and do as you're fucking told.

THOMAS. Sure I was only talking to him yesterday about how he fucking hated touts.

FATHER. That's easy enough to say.

THOMAS. You need to open the window. There's a smell in here.

THOMAS *goes into the bedroom.*

FATHER. Sorry about that, JJ. He's been acting that way since his brother. Of course the whole thing is my fault.

JJ. How long has it been?

FATHER. Hold on for a second. (*Shouts down hallway.*) And don't you be fucking earwiggin', Thomas! Do you hear me? We're havin' a meetin'!

THOMAS (*offstage*). Go fuck yourself.

FATHER. I'll come down there and give you 'Go fuck yourself' in a minute. You just stay in your fuckin' wormhole until I tell you to come out. Do you hear me? (*To* JJ.) Fucking little cunt. Sorry, where was I, JJ?

JJ. I was askin' you how long it's been, Joe?

FATHER *is lost.*

Since your other son died.

FATHER. Oh that's right. Sorry. Let me see: over a year. We had the anniversary mass last month.

JJ *nods.*

He's been mopin' around like that since it happened. You have to move on. Go on livin'. That's what I keep on tellin' him. But sure does he fuckin' listen? I know they were close but sure fuck it, I was the boy's father. I wish to God it hadn't happened either but sure there you go, these things happen. And maybe they happen for a reason. I don't know. Some people say it's unnatural but sure I think it's the most natural thing in the world if you look at it a certain way.

JJ. How's that Joe?

FATHER. Well, it's like cattle, JJ. God forgive me for sayin' this but it's like cullin' a herd a cattle. It's natural. If cattle weren't killed, sure they'd be throwing themselves into the river an' all. It's the natural order. But sure what can I do? It's not my fault. I didn't have a fucking magic wand.

JJ. How are you holdin' up yourself, Joe?

FATHER. Not too bad, JJ. Thanks for askin'. I'm all right. I suppose. Sometimes I do lose the head with young Thomas there and he's a good boy. There's no harm in him.

JJ. He's a good lad. Is he?

FATHER. Oh he is. Solid! 100 per cent!

JJ. He seems solid enough.

FATHER. Oh he is. He is indeed. No doubt about that!

JJ. You found him yourself?

FATHER. Shamey? I did. I found him right enough. Said he was going fishing. Had the rods out with him and all, boy. He even packed fucking sandwiches. Fucking sandwiches! Can you believe that, hi?

JJ. How did you find him?

FATHER. Sure I saw him jump in. I was a couple of hundred yards from him. Saw him do it.

JJ. There was nothing you could do?

FATHER. No! Not wan thing! Sure if I'd a been able to swim that would have been something. I would have jumped straight in. But be the time I got up there it was too late. He'd done the deed. We couldn't find the body for three days. Be rights we should have had a closed coffin but sure the mother insisted on seein' him in it. (*Pause.*) The tablets were no good at all after that. Didn't seem to work. Made her worse if you ask me. But you just have to get on with it.

JJ. That's the truth, Joe.

FATHER. Oh it is surely, JJ. It is surely. But Thomas seems to think it affects no-one only himself.

JJ. Would he not talk to you about it?

FATHER. No, sure you see yourself the way he is. There's no talking to him.

JJ. Well I saw him down in the yard in deep conversation with that other dopey cunt.

FATHER. Barney?

JJ. Aye.

FATHER. Well he won't say anything to him if that's what you're worried about. He'll say nothing to Barney, JJ. I'll make sure a that. Himself and Barney do get on. That's a fact. But if Barney's our boy, you'll get no trouble from Tommy. You can be sure of that.

JJ. You're sure of that?

FATHER. Oh that's wan thing you can be sure of.

Pause. JJ *stands.*

JJ. We'll start work on him when I get back.

FATHER. What do you want me to do?

JJ. Get the shed ready and that'll do. Don't say a fucking word. And I'll be back with the boys tomorrow.

FATHER *nods.* JJ *exits.* FATHER *waits for a few moments.*

FATHER (*calls*). Thomas! Thomas! I need a word. Thomas!

THOMAS *enters.*

THOMAS. What?

FATHER. What do you mean, what?

THOMAS. What the fuck are you telling that cunt that Barney's a fucking tout. He's not a fucking tout.

FATHER. I didn't say he was.

THOMAS. Well you seem to have convinced your man that you think he is.

FATHER. I think he might be, but I'm not sure.

THOMAS. There's no way is Barney a tout.

FATHER. Thomas, listen we need to look into this. We've gone over everything and all I can say is that I'm not 100 per cent confident in him.

THOMAS. Could it not just be high-tech surveillance and they want us to think that it's Barney?

FATHER. Could well be.

THOMAS. So why hasn't the full nutting squad been called in?

FATHER. Because JJ is the nutting squad.

THOMAS. I thought he'd have deputies; there'd be a court martial?

FATHER. That'll come later. But JJ likes to make his mind up first.

THOMAS. And has he made up his mind? Has he?

FATHER. No.

THOMAS. And where's he gone now . . . What happens if Barney says he's a tout and he's not?

FATHER. That won't happen.

THOMAS. If the boys go to work on him it might.

FATHER. It won't. I'll be there. I'll make sure of that. There's no way Barney's gettin' stiffed on my watch if he's not the informer.

THOMAS. Your man hasn't made up his mind.

FATHER. No, he hasn't. He thinks it might be something as simple as a failed battery pack. These things happen.

THOMAS. You'd tell me if he had.

FATHER. Sure why would I lie? Nothing will happen unless I'm 100 per cent sure, boy.

THOMAS. Because there's no way I'm lettin' anything happen to Barney.

FATHER. If Barney's the tout, you'll do nothing only follow orders, boy.

THOMAS. I won't.

FATHER. You will, boy. Because if Barney is the tout, then he was the man could have got you or me killed or locked up any number of times. Don't forget that.

THOMAS. But how could Barney do that? I've known him since I was a young fella.

FATHER. Touts don't think of the consequences of touting. They tout and everything that happens as a result of that, they tell themselves it's not their fault, somebody else did it. It's never their fault.

THOMAS. It's not Barney.

FATHER. Well let's be sure it's not.

THOMAS. It's not.

FATHER. This is simply a safety precaution. No-one likes a tout hunt. But these things need to be done.

THOMAS. But you were the one called JJ in?

FATHER. I had to.

THOMAS. You had to?

FATHER. Aye, I had to. If I hadn't called him in then, the Boss man would have called him in.

THOMAS. So?

FATHER. So then it might not be only Barney they'd be asking questions of.

THOMAS. What do you mean?

FATHER. I'm sayin' this way at least I might be able to control it.

THOMAS. What's to control? If there's a tout, there's a tout.

FATHER *is looking at him.*

What do you mean? Do you think it's me? How the fuck could you think that?

FATHER. I don't think that.

THOMAS. Well what then?

FATHER. Nothing. It doesn't matter. All I'm sayin' is things can go wrong when you don't have control. That's why I was the wan called JJ in. To have control.

THOMAS. So?

FATHER. So what?

THOMAS. Do you have control?

FATHER. We'll see.

THOMAS. We'll see? That's it.

FATHER. That's it.

THOMAS *shakes his head and goes back to his bedroom.*
FATHER *stays at the table, staring ahead.*

Fade to black.

Scene Five

BARNEY *and* UNKNOWN MAN *in a car park / anonymous urban setting.*

BARNEY. Joe's smiling at me all the time. It's like he knows.

MAN. You need to take it easy, Barney.

BARNEY. Fuck you. Easy for you to say. I can tell the way Joe is looking at me, he fucking thinks it's me.

MAN. If he thought it was you, Barney, me and you wouldn't be having this conversation, would we?

BARNEY. I'm telling you now he does. He thinks it's me. He thinks I'm the informer.

MAN. Well tell him you're not.

BARNEY. He thinks I am.

MAN. Well you're not.

BARNEY. Aye, but sure –

MAN. That's what you need to get into your head. You're not.

BARNEY *sighs.*

BARNEY. How come you fuckers didn't let that bomb go off?

MAN. We can't let a bomb like that go off, Barney. You know that.

BARNEY. You've done it before.

MAN. No, we haven't, Barney.

BARNEY. Go on outa that! That's me rightly fucked now. They'll fuckin' blame me.

MAN. Barney, listen to me, if we thought you were compromised, in any way, I'd have you out of here right this minute.

Pause.

Barney, your safety is our primary concern.

BARNEY *is staring into space.*

We couldn't let a bomb go off. Listen, Barney; you're an invaluable asset to us. Look at me, Barney. Look at me. Nothing bad will happen to you. You have to trust me. Do you believe me?

BARNEY. How the fuck would I believe you? And how could I trust you? Sure how do you know what they know? How do you know what goes on in Joe's head? You don't. So don't tell me, take her hand, Barney, nothing will happen to you. 'Cause you fucking don't know that. Only God knows. And you're not fucking God. Am I right?

MAN. No, I'm not.

BARNEY. Of course you're not. You're not God is right.

MAN. All I'm saying, Barney, is your safety is our highest priority.

BARNEY. Me fucking hole. You couldn't give a fuck. I'm like your fucking soldiers. Fucking cannon fodder!

MAN. Well, it was your decision, Barney.

BARNEY. It wasn't. Youse put fucking pressure on me to sign that fucking thing.

MAN. Well, you could have taken your chances, Barney. You chose not to.

BARNEY. I should have listened to Joe. Say nothing, he was always saying. Don't say a fucking thing. Pick a spot on the wall and keep looking at it. Let your mind go blank. And these fuckers are like, hey Barney, where's the spot on the wall? Think we don't know about the spot on the wall, Barney. Show us the spot on the wall, Barney. Is this the spot? Where's the spot? Think we won't tell Joe you're a fuckin' tout, Barney. Let you out fuckin' early, Barney. Then he'll think you're a tout. Barney the tout. Keep looking at the wall, Barney. Keep lookin' at that spot, Barney. And I couldn't fucking concentrate. I had my spot on the wall picked out. And I can't fucking see it. And I'm thinkin' Joe's been acting horrid quare lately. And I'm thinkin' these fuckers will set me up. And they fuckin' did. They set me up rightly.

MAN. They didn't, Barney. You talked.

BARNEY. And I'll tell you this much for nothing. I wish I fucking hadn't.

MAN. Barney, let me say this. You've crossed over the line. There's no going back. You think if you say, sorry boys, I've been an informer for the last year, but I'm back, they'll accept that. You think they'll just forgive you and wipe the slate clean.

BARNEY *doesn't say a word.*

Because they won't, Barney. And it's no use thinking you can shop us either. That won't work. You know that. Barney! Do you know that?

BARNEY. I know that.

MAN. This will only work if there's trust.

BARNEY. I just think my time is up. It's like a big black crow sittin' on my shoulder. That Belfast fella has already decided I'm for the cross.

MAN. Barney, that's the one way you will end up dead. Thinking like that.

BARNEY. I need to get out.

MAN. You need to keep it together, Barney.

BARNEY. Well tell me this then. Why's that fella down from Belfast?

MAN. Barney, we've already been over this.

BARNEY. Well I want to go over it again.

MAN. Do you need some money?

BARNEY. I don't want your fucking money. I want out.

MAN. Whatever you want, Barney. If you want out, we'll get you out.

BARNEY. Well I want out then.

MAN. Barney . . .

Silence.

BARNEY. I want to go someplace.

MAN. Where do you want to go? A housing estate in Milton
   Keynes? Is that what you want?

BARNEY. Where's that?

MAN. It's outside London.

BARNEY. I don't want to go to London.

MAN. Well where then, Barney?

BARNEY. Australia!

MAN. Australia?

BARNEY. Aye, Australia. I hear it's warm there. (*Laughs.*)

MAN. Australia! Fine. (*Laughs. Pause.*) Barney, you said
   yourself if they thought it was you, you'd be dead by now.

BARNEY. I would?

MAN. You would.

BARNEY. So what are they at?

MAN. I don't know. That's what I want you to find out.

BARNEY. Did I tell you even young Tommy was looking at
   me crossways yesterday?

MAN. Why was that?

BARNEY. I was being a fucking eegit. He started quizzin'
   me on what went through me head after bein' lifted and
   I started – fuck me – harping on about that fella, the last
   fella that got shot and left out be the cross. I shouldn't a
   opened me mouth. I might as well have a big sign on me
   back saying 'Barney's the fuckin' tout. Barney is the
   informer.' (*Starts laughing.*) I mean I've seen fellas with
   half their heads blown off and bits of brain and blood and
   it doesn't bother me. And wan time I saw a fucking ribcage

of a fucking solider and a fucking bird, a big black crow gnawing at it. And I didn't give a fuck. And there I am fucking thinking about this poor useless fuck and his bare feet and tellin' young Tommy about it.

MAN. If you think about it, Barney, that's the last thing a tout would be talking about.

BARNEY. That's not the point . . . Tommy. Me and Tommy. He's like a lost, a little lost lamb and I don't want to see anything happen to him. Have you got that?

MAN. I hear you, Barney. I hear you. But what about that fella from Belfast?

BARNEY. What about him?

MAN. We'll have him lifted on the way back to Belfast.

BARNEY. Jesus Christ, don't do that. You might as well put that tout sign on me back straight away. 'Informer at work!' That's a good wan! Hah! (*Laughs.*) Informer at work!

MAN. If we don't lift him, Barney, he'll be wondering why we didn't.

BARNEY. Well lift away then. Lift away.

Fade to black.

Scene Six

The next day. THOMAS *is in the kitchen.* JJ *knocks on the back door and enters.*

THOMAS. JJ.

JJ. Thomas.

THOMAS. The aul fella's over in the shed the other side of the yard.

JJ. I know he is.

THOMAS. He is. Do you want me to bring you over?

JJ. No, I think I might be able to find my own way over there without too much trouble. But thanks for the offer, Tommy.

THOMAS. That's alright.

JJ. So what about Barney?

THOMAS. What about him?

JJ. What about him? How long would you say Barney's worked around here?

THOMAS. It's not Barney.

JJ. I didn't say it was.

THOMAS. Well it's not.

JJ. I didn't ask you if you thought it was Barney. All I asked you was how long he's worked around here.

THOMAS. I don't – What's this got to do with me?

JJ. Everything.

THOMAS. Why don't you talk to the old man about this?

JJ. I did and now I'm talking to you.

THOMAS *nods.*

So how long has Barney worked around here?

THOMAS. As long as I can remember. Years.

JJ. What does he do?

THOMAS. Odd jobs around the place.

JJ. Odd jobs? That's fair enough.

THOMAS. You know, like the milking, repairing fences, drivin' tractors.

JJ. Drivin' tractors?

THOMAS. Yea.

JJ. Is drivin' a tractor more or less the same as a car?

THOMAS. More or less.

JJ. What would I have to know now if I was driving a tractor? Or could I just start her up and away I go?

THOMAS. No, it's different with a tractor. Once you take your foot off the clutch, she goes. She wouldn't conk out, so she wouldn't.

JJ. Would she not?

THOMAS. No.

JJ. And do you not need a foot on the accelerator then if you don't have a foot on the clutch?

THOMAS. No.

JJ. So Barney drives the tractor?

THOMAS. Sometimes. What about him anyway?

JJ. You tell me?

THOMAS. He's not the tout if that's what you're thinking.

JJ. I'm not thinking anything.

THOMAS. Well why ask me questions about Barney?

JJ. Your father thinks it's Barney.

THOMAS. How could it be Barney? Barney doesn't know fuck. He's fucking dumb.

JJ. Most fucking touts are dumb. That's how they get caught. Where is Barney when there's meetings on here?

THOMAS. I'm not fucking shopping Barney. 'Cause I'm telling you. It's not him.

JJ (*softly*). I need to fucking know, kid, OK? You're in a fucking army. I'm giving you a fucking order. Where is Barney when there's meetings on here?

THOMAS. You heard it all from my father. Why the fuck do you need to talk to me?

JJ. Because this is a fucking war. There's people's lives at stake here.

Pause.

What happened at the last meeting?

Pause.

THOMAS. We were in the kitchen, we were going through plans for an operation – and one of the boys heard a noise from the scullery.

JJ. And what was it?

THOMAS. I went out to look and there was nothing. It could have been one of the dogs.

JJ. And where was Barney?

THOMAS. Barney was in the yard. Tidying up, that kind a thing.

JJ. But you think Barney was listening?

THOMAS. No, I think he was – I think he just wanted to be around us.

JJ. Sneakin' around you.

THOMAS. No!

JJ. Do you think Barney feels left out?

THOMAS. Sometimes.

JJ. You think Barney doesn't like bein' a messenger boy?

THOMAS. Sure Barney knows it's on a need-to-know basis. He knows, he knows what the score is.

JJ. What does he know?

THOMAS. Barney knew fuck all about that operation beforehand. In fact, he knew nothing. Barney does what he's told.

JJ. He knew something. He knew you were having a meeting.

THOMAS. It wouldn't take a fucking rocket scientist to work that one out. But he didn't know it was for something planned the following day.

JJ. Of course he did.

THOMAS. How would he have known if nobody had told him?

JJ. We don't know that nobody told him.

THOMAS. Well nobody told him. It was watertight.

JJ. And what happened?

THOMAS. We were going to go ahead with it. Everything was fucking ready. Scouts had gone on ahead. Clear path in, clear path out.

JJ. But it didn't go ahead?

THOMAS. No.

JJ. Why not?

THOMAS. The auld fella said he thought there was something wrong.

JJ. What was wrong?

THOMAS. He didn't know. Said he could smell something in the air. Too quiet! No helicopters, no nothing. There was something wrong. He has a fucking sixth sense about things like that, the aul fella. He can smell the air and know if there's fucking trouble.

JJ. So what happened?

THOMAS. So we abandoned the operation and that was that.

JJ. And that was that?

THOMAS. That was that.

JJ. Do you think your father was right to cancel the operation?

THOMAS. Of course.

JJ. Of course is right. What about the bomb attack on the barracks?

THOMAS. What about it?

JJ. The bomb didn't go off.

THOMAS. Sure you know that sometimes happens.

JJ. They lifted Barney afterwards.

THOMAS. Barney was held for the seven days same as everyone else.

JJ. Bar your father. Why do you think your father thinks it's Barney?

THOMAS. Why don't you ask him that?

JJ. I did ask him. Now I'm askin' you.

THOMAS. I don't think it's Barney.

JJ. I didn't ask you that. I asked you why do you think your father thinks it's Barney.

THOMAS. I don't know. If he thinks that, he's wrong.

JJ. Listen Tommy, open your fucking mind! Okay? I'm not saying it is Barney. But think! If not Barney, then who?

THOMAS. It's not Barney!

JJ. Could it be your father?

THOMAS. No! Sure how the fuck would it be him?

JJ. What about you? You were lifted for the seven days.

THOMAS. I was.

JJ. What did you say to them?

THOMAS. I already went over this when I was debriefed.

JJ. And they let your father out after 48 hours. Why?

THOMAS. So they could give fuckheads like you something to do.

JJ. Don't be acting like a fucking girl. If Barney's the informer then he's fucking dead and that's that.

THOMAS. If it's Barney, I'll do him myself.

JJ. You won't be doin' anybody yourself. All you have to do is answer my questions.

THOMAS. I'm just saying whoever it is, it's not Barney.

JJ. Well your father seems to think it is . . . (*Pause.*) OK, I want to go over everything with you again. We'll start with the arrest.

Fade to black.

Scene Seven

A body with a black plastic bag over the head on one side of stage. Body in awkward position. Blood. No shoes or socks. Shirt half-off, belly exposed. Hands tied behind back.

BARNEY's voice is heard on a scratchy-sounding tape. His voice breaks down repeatedly. At times he appears to be reading from a prepared script.

VOICE OF BARNEY. I am very sorry . . . for all that I have done. I am . . . an informer . . . and have been passing information on . . . to the Crown forces . . . that has endangered the lives of volunteers. I fully . . .

I'm sorry . . . Please fucking . . . I fully accept responsibility for my actions and I have not made this confession under, under duress. I'm sorry. I broke. Me. They . . . That's all . . . I don't – I didn't take any money. Not wan penny! I would not do that. I, I . . . They said they would have set me up and say I was an informer anyway. I don't . . . I didn't . . . I don't . . . know . . . I didn't want to. I want to apologise to my former comrades. I am . . . most heartily sorry . . . for all that I have done . . . I want to apologise to my . . . family for becoming . . . what is the lowest of the low. (*Breathing heavily.*) I know . . . my mother and father will meet me in . . . Heaven and . . . I pray that . . . that they will not be ashamed of me. I pray and trust in God Almighty and Powerful that they will see it in their hearts to forgive a wayward son of Ireland. I pray that they will meet me there, there, their, their loving son, Barney.

Long pause.

I forgive those who will soon send me to . . . to my death . . .
I know, I know that they are only doing their duty . . . If
there's wan thing I regret is that, that I, I wanted to die the
death of a volunteer . . . a soldier . . . but because of my
own actions I know . . . I know I will now suffer the fate of
all informers.

May God have mercy on my soul.

Fade to black.

Scene Eight

The interior of a shed. THOMAS *is crying.* FATHER *enters and
drops a black plastic bag in front of* THOMAS. *It is wet.*
FATHER *starts cleaning up.*

FATHER. That's enough of this shite. What's done is done. I
    want you to take this bag and bury it out the back.

THOMAS. What's in it?

FATHER. A couple of mongrel pups. I'm only after drowndin'
    them.

THOMAS. You drownded them, you bury them!

FATHER. I'm fucking tellin' you now, boy. Take that bag and
    bury it out the fuckin' back. I have enough on me plate.

THOMAS. You fuckin' bury them.

FATHER. I won't tell you again.

THOMAS. What are you going to do? Do me as well?

FATHER. That wasn't my decision.

THOMAS. No?

FATHER. The man had a fair court martial. He was a tout.
    It's a good job we found him when we did or where would
    we be?

THOMAS. He was your friend.

FATHER. He was not. He was not my fucking friend. He was a bastard tout fucking cunt bastard. I should never have trusted him. Him bein' what he was. And not even a fuckin' local. And me takin' him in and giving him a job. Eaten bread is soon forgot.

THOMAS. What do you mean? Him bein' what he was?

FATHER. He was a fuckin *shut-in* from Inniskeen. Nobody knew that now. I didn't mention it to a soul and that's how he repaid me.

THOMAS. A shuteen?

FATHER. A fuckin' *shut-in*. A fella that's shut in. An inbred. His father and mother were brother and sister. He was the only child. A fuckin' shut-in from down this side of Inniskeen.

THOMAS. What the fuck does that matter?

FATHER. It's abnormal. It's against nature. Fucking animals wouldn't do that.

THOMAS. What's that got to do with Barney bein' a tout?

FATHER. Sure they have ways of getting to people like Barney.

THOMAS. And you're saying the Brits knew this about Barney?

FATHER. How the fuck would I know? . . . If only his mother and father had given him a sister, sure Barney could have married her himself and they could have spawned a half a dozen little fuckin' shut-in cunt bastards between the two a them. (*Laughs.*)

THOMAS. He had a second cousin in Clones, so he did. She used to have him over for the dinner once in a while, he said.

FATHER. There was no cousin in Clones. He made that up. Sure what person in their right mind would admit to bein' related to something like that? There was no cousin. And it's a good job there was no cousin. She'd only a bin shamed havin' a tout in the family.

THOMAS. But how was Barney a tout?

FATHER. Sure what makes a man do anything?

THOMAS. What did he say at the end?

FATHER. Sure what could he say?

THOMAS. Did he say he was the tout?

FATHER. He did.

THOMAS. What did he say?

FATHER. He told us he was the tout.

THOMAS. But what did he say?

FATHER. He was sayin' lots of things. He was squealing like a fucking sick calf lookin' for its mother.

THOMAS. What did you do with him?

FATHER. What do you mean, what did we do with him? We put a bullet in the back of his head.

THOMAS. No, I mean what did you do with him after?

FATHER. We dumped him on the road. Down at the cross. The road the other side of the cross.

THOMAS. Bag over his head?

FATHER. Of course bag over his head.

THOMAS. What type of bag?

FATHER. What kind of bag do you think? A fucking handbag. A black plastic bag. Two of them and I tied it around the neck with masking tape.

THOMAS. Like this bag. (*Picks up the bag of pups.*)

FATHER. What are you doing? A black plastic bag is a black plastic bag.

THOMAS. A doggy bag?

FATHER. A black plastic fucking bag and no more.

THOMAS. Shoes on or off?

FATHER. What?

THOMAS. Shoes on or off? Did ye leave the shoes on him or did you dump him barefoot?

FATHER. What does it matter?

THOMAS. Shoes on or off?

FATHER. We took the shoes off him. They were the work boots he always wears. We let him keep the socks on though.

THOMAS. You let him keep the socks on?

FATHER. We did. Full of holes they were. His big toe and half his fuckin' foot sticking out. Sure what difference does it make if he had his socks off or on? He was a tout.

THOMAS. He wasn't.

FATHER. What do you mean he wasn't? Sure we have his confession on tape.

THOMAS *is silent for a few moments staring at his* FATHER.

THOMAS. I know it's you.

FATHER. Me?

THOMAS. You're the tout.

FATHER. What the fuck are you on about?

THOMAS. You're the fuckin' tout. I fuckin' know.

FATHER (*picking up spade*). Is this about Shamey?

THOMAS. What do you mean?

FATHER. Nothing.

THOMAS. What's Shamey got to do with it?

FATHER. Shamey was sick is all.

THOMAS. What did you mean Shamey was sick?

FATHER. I didn't mean anything only he was not well.

THOMAS. You think Shamey said something to me?

FATHER. Don't be getting carried away with yourself, son. Shamey was sick. That's all.

THOMAS. Shut the fuck up talking about my brother, you fucking tout cunt.

FATHER. Watch your mouth, Tommy.

THOMAS. Or what?

FATHER. Or you'll have a . . . a fucking accident that's what'll happen.

THOMAS. An accident. Just like Shamey?

FATHER. Listen . . . son. You're upset. I don't know why Shamey done what he done. I'm not the informer. Barney was.

THOMAS. Oh Barney was. Was he?

FATHER. He admitted it all. We have his full confession on tape, so we do. We do indeed.

THOMAS. Oh that's handy enough. That is. And tell me this, *cunt*, why have you got that spade in your hand? What are you going to do? Hit me across the back of the head; dump me in the river?

FATHER. Don't be sayin' things like that now. Sure I saw Shamey after drowndin' himself with my own eyes.

THOMAS. Then why have you got a spade in your hand?

FATHER. Here, take the fucking spade. (*Throws him the spade.*) I don't want the spade.

THOMAS *catches the spade. Throws it back to him.*

THOMAS. No, you take the spade. I want to see what accident it is you have in store for me.

FATHER. No, you take it. (*Throws spade back.*) I didn't mean that. It was only for burying that bag a pups. We have Barney's confession on tape, so we do.

THOMAS. So you keep sayin'. So Shamey reckoned you were a tout.

FATHER. Shamey fuckin'made things up. I'm after tellin' you. He was sick in the head.

THOMAS. I told you, don't talk about my brother, *cunt*.

FATHER. Well whatever he told you, it was a lie.

THOMAS. I'll tell you again, don't talk about my brother, *cunt*.

FATHER. Sure how can I answer accusations from a dead man. It's wan thing –

THOMAS *hits his* FATHER *with the spade.* FATHER *goes down on his knees.*

Ah Jasus, what the fuck have you done?

THOMAS. It was JJ told me he thought you were the tout, not Shamey.

FATHER. JJ? What do you mean?

THOMAS. JJ.

FATHER. I don't understand.

THOMAS. You think JJ and the Boss man is fucking eegits. You thought Barney gets done and that's that.

FATHER. I don't –

THOMAS. Calling JJ in yourself. Nice touch. He liked that. Come on, how long have you been at it?

FATHER. Thomas, son, please!

THOMAS. Please what?

FATHER. That last bomb that didn't go off. Barney admitted he had it fixed himself.

THOMAS. That was a set-up, wasn't it?

FATHER. How the fuck would it be a set-up?

THOMAS. The last six months you've been tryin' to set him up. 'I smell something in the air.' Of course you smelt it. It was you.

FATHER. Son, this is fucking Boss-man crazy talk. I'm not a fuckin' tout!

THOMAS. Of course you're not.

FATHER. I'm not!

THOMAS. When you were arrested at Easter two years ago? You didn't mention it to anybody. Barney knew though. Told me about it!

FATHER *says nothing. Silence.*

Why did you say to Barney, to keep an eye on us if anything happened to you? What did you think was going to happen to you?

FATHER. For fuck's sake. All that happened was a branch man stuck his fuckin' gun in my mouth. I was a bit shook up was all.

THOMAS. Why didn't you tell anybody else about this?

FATHER. Sure what could I say? The fuck puts a gun in my mouth and I shat myself? That doesn't look too good.

THOMAS. You set Barney up?

FATHER. Barney was a fucking tout.

THOMAS. Maybe he was.

FATHER. He was. I know he was.

THOMAS. Did your Brit friends tell you he was? . . .

FATHER *says nothing.*

They fucking did. Barney was a tout. But so are you. You get the Brits to finger you, so even the Boss man thinks you're clean. You're some fucking cunt. I bet the fuckin' Brits knew you were settin' up Barney? Am I right? You and the Brits settin' up Barney.

FATHER. That's Boss-man talk now that is.

THOMAS. Is it?

FATHER. That's right. Fucking paranoia.

THOMAS. Well what about Easter two years ago? You got fuckin' lifted and said nothing to nobody.

FATHER. Sure I told you already Barney knew. Sure what had I to hide?

THOMAS. Did Shamey know?

FATHER. Did Shamey know what?

THOMAS. Did Shamey know that you were touting?

FATHER. Jesus Christ, Thomas. This is what I warned you about. What did I say? Try and fuckin' take control, otherwise things will go wrong.

THOMAS. Well why did you say what you said about Shamey?

FATHER. What did I say?

THOMAS. You know what you said. You said Shamey was a liar. Why did you say that?

FATHER. But Barney admitted –

THOMAS. I don't give a fuck what Barney said. Why did you say that about Shamey?

FATHER *says nothing.*

I'll count to three otherwise I'll take the fucking head off you with this spade. Did you drown Shamey?

FATHER. Ah for fuck's sake, son.

THOMAS. Well something happened. A year before he died. Shamey was acting odd since then. That year before he died. What happened? Did Shamey know you were a tout?

FATHER. I didn't kill Shamey.

THOMAS. Did you kill him?

FATHER. Jesus Christ, son, what do you think? I'd kill my own son?

THOMAS. You killed Barney.

FATHER. That was different. It was JJ's call.

THOMAS. And you had no say in the matter?

FATHER. It was JJ's call.

THOMAS. That's funny because JJ says you were the one tried to shoot him before the questioning was over.

FATHER. That's fuckin' horseshit. I scalped him a bit is all. It was an accident.

THOMAS. An accident?

FATHER. It was an accident. And sure no harm was done the man till he had that confession signed. And we had everything down on paper.

THOMAS. Will you fuckin' listen to yourself? A minute ago you were tellin' me how it had to be done. Why?

FATHER *is silent.*

Come on, give me a fuckin' answer. Did Shamey know you were a tout?

A long silence. Suddenly, as if he is very tired, FATHER *speaks.*

FATHER. No.

THOMAS. Did you push Shamey in?

FATHER. No.

THOMAS. Then what?

Silence again. Longer this time.

FATHER. He knew.

THOMAS. He knew. That's all I wanted to know. What happened?

FATHER. I don't know. He knew, that's all. I told him he was imagining things and he looked at me funny. That's why I said what I said to Barney.

THOMAS. You fuckin' tout.

FATHER. I just broke. That's all there was to it.

THOMAS. Fuckin' tout.

FATHER. There were asking me questions and I got this fuzzy feeling in my head, I thought I was going mad. Didn't understand it. I had to fuckin' get out of there.

THOMAS. Did you sign a statement?

FATHER. I gave them the whole fuckin' shop, boy! And then there was no goin' back.

THOMAS *is silent.*

Where's JJ now?

THOMAS. You know where he is. He's up at the house.

FATHER. He doesn't know. There's no proof.

THOMAS. There's your confession to me.

FATHER. Is there a way out of this, son? Me getting lifted two years ago. No-one knows that, only Barney.

THOMAS. And me.

FATHER. And you.

Pause.

THOMAS. Listen do me a favour, boy, and save your breath for JJ.

FATHER. Son? I –

THOMAS. Shut up, cunt.

FATHER. Son, believe me. I wish what happened to Shamey hadn't a happened. Sometimes things just happen.

THOMAS. Take your shoes and socks off. (*Picks up the spade.*) Hurry the fuck up. Who left this spade here? Which one of youse little cunts left this spade here? I'll ask you again. Who left the fucking spade out here?

FATHER. I had nothing to do with Shamey, son. I saw it happen and it . . . (*Pause.*) . . . it broke my heart.

THOMAS. I didn't ask you about Shamey. I asked you about the fucking spade.

FATHER. He done that on his own accord. He wasn't my fault.

THOMAS *kicks him in the stomach.*

THOMAS. I said not to talk about my brother, *cunt.* Now I won't tell you again. Take off your shoes and socks. Now!

FATHER *begins with difficulty to take off his boots.*

FATHER. Is there no way?

THOMAS. Jesus Christ, you're like all same, touts. (*Mimics.*) Is there no way? Take off your shoes and socks.

FATHER *takes off both boots and one sock. That's enough for* THOMAS. *He savagely hits his* FATHER *across the head. He turns him over. He sits on his back. He takes some masking tape and starts to wrap it around the* FATHER*'s wrists. Stands up and looks at his handiwork. There's one thing left.* THOMAS *takes the black plastic bag, empties out the dead pups. He puts the bag on his* FATHER*'s head and wraps it around the neck with masking tape.*

Cunt.

Fade to black.

Scene Nine

A year later. The kitchen again.

THOMAS *comes into the empty kitchen in a hurry. He's wearing a blue boiler suit, surgical gloves. He takes the gloves off and throws them into the Stanley cooker. He unbuttons the top of his boiler suit and takes his T-shirt off. Underneath his T-shirt, there is a piece of foam on the right side of his chest attached with masking tape. He pulls it off, winces and throws it in the stove.*

He takes a big pot of boiling water off the top of the cooker and takes it into the scullery. He pours the hot water into the scullery sink. He strips off and puts his clothes into the washing machine. He pours the washing powder in the machine, then pours it over himself. Sets the washing machine on and puts shampoo on his head. Then he starts scrubbing himself, paying particular attention to his hands. He half-rinses himself off, and goes through the kitchen and into the bedroom.

DANNY *comes in, dumps his schoolbag down and turns on the TV.*

THOMAS *comes back in, wearing tracksuit trousers and a T-shirt. He looks like he's out of the shower. He's drying his hair with a small towel.*

THOMAS. How was school, son?

DANNY. The usual.

THOMAS. The usual? So what's the plan, boy?

DANNY. No plan. Watch the telly.

THOMAS. Do you want to play one of your games? Turn off the telly and we'll play one of your games.

DANNY. I don't play games anymore, Tommy. I keep tellin' you that. I'm too old for games.

THOMAS. Sorry, Danny. I'm only trying to do the best I can for youse. The best I can. You know that. Do you not believe me?

DANNY *doesn't say anything.*

I'm going up to see your mother at the weekend if you want to come.

DANNY. No, I'll stay here.

THOMAS. Do you not want to see your mother?

DANNY. No, I don't want to go up there.

THOMAS. She'll be home soon I think. The last time I was up there, doctor said the new tablets were working much better. She'll be back home to us in no time.

DANNY. I'm going off to the cousin's house. I'll see you later.

DANNY *exits.* THOMAS *looks at the picture of Shamey.*

THOMAS. Oh that's right she'll be back home to us soon enough. When will she back, says you? Soon, says I. How soon says you? Oh soon enough, soon enough. Soon enough is right. The mother will be back. Back where she belongs. And then we'll all be together again. (*Gets upset. Picks up the picture.*) And we'll all be fine, Shamey. You and me and Danny and Mammy. We'll all be fine . . . Only we're not fine are we, Shamey? I'm not fine. No, not by a long shot.

So where's God in all of this Shamey? My brother Shamey. My brother. My brother is dead. My dead brother. Dead brother. Dead. Died. Two years since my brother died.

Are you a ghost now, Shamey? Is your spirit wandering around the place unhappy and sad, not knowing who it is? Faint memories of who you used to be and the people who loved you. Because I loved you, Shamey. I loved you and if you're a ghost or a spirit who forgot that once you used to be my brother Shamey, then wake up! That's who you are, my brother, my brother Shamey, that I love. Spirit, can you hear me? You are my brother Shamey, Tommy's brother Shamey that he loves.

When you died, Shamey, I would take your clothes and bury my head in them and close my eyes to catch the smell of you. Like the footprints of a ghost. Hold on to your T-shirt like a sick babby's sucky blanket. And furrow my brow so I looked like you and looking back in the mirror it was almost you, a ghost of you. A trace of you. You, my brother, my dear gentle dead brother. Tommy loves his brother.

THOMAS *goes down under kitchen table. He curls up in the foetal position. Light slowly fades.*

Enter DANNY. *He goes into the bedroom, then comes back out. Is about to turn on the telly when he notices* THOMAS *underneath the kitchen table.*

DANNY (*concerned*). Tommy, what are you doing? What's the matter? Tommy! (*Gets down on his knees and gives him a gentle shake.*) Thomas, wake up! Thomas, don't be scarin' me.

THOMAS. Shamey?

DANNY. No, it's Danny.

THOMAS (*sleepily*). Danny?

DANNY. It's me, Danny . . . Are you okay?

THOMAS. I'm all right. I'm asleep.

DANNY. What are you doing?

THOMAS. I'm asleep. Shamey's in my dream, boy. We're having an adventure.

DANNY *gets a blanket and two cushions from the settee and puts the cushions underneath* THOMAS'*s head and covers him with the blanket. He lies down on the floor beside* THOMAS. *They are head to head.*

Fade to black.

The End.

A Nick Hern Book

Defender of the Faith first published in Great Britain
as a paperback original in 2004 by Nick Hern Books Limited,
14 Larden Road, London W3 7ST in association with
the Abbey Theatre, Dublin

Defender of the Faith copyright © 2004 Stuart Carolan

Stuart Carolan has asserted his right to be identified
as the author of this work

Cover image: Zeus Creative Consultants

Typeset by Country Setting, Kingsdown, Kent CT14 8ES
Printed and bound in Great Britain by Cox and Wyman Limited,
Reading, Berks

A CIP catalogue record for this book is available from
the British Library

ISBN 1 85459 816 3

CAUTION   All rights whatsoever in this play are strictly
reserved. Requests to reproduce the text in whole or in part should
be addressed to the publisher.

Amateur Performing Rights   Applications for performance,
including readings and excerpts, by amateurs in English throughout
the world should be addressed to the Performing Rights Manager,
Nick Hern Books, 14 Larden Road, London W3 7ST, *fax*
+44 (0)20 8735 0250, *e-mail* info@nickhernbooks.demon.co.uk,
except as follows:

Australia: Dominie Drama, 8 Cross Street, Brookvale 2100,
fax (2) 9905 5209, *e-mail* dominie@dominie.com.au

New Zealand: Play Bureau, PO Box 420, New Plymouth,
fax (6) 753 2150, *e-mail* play.bureau.nz@xtra.co.nz

United States of America and Canada: Peter Strauss, Rogers,
Coleridge and White Ltd, 20 Powis Mews, London W11 1JN,
fax +44 (0)20 7229 9084

Professional Performing Rights   Applications for performance
by professionals in any medium and in any language throughout
the world should be addressed to Peter Strauss, Rogers, Coleridge
and White Ltd, 20 Powis Mews, London W11 1JN,
fax +44 (0)20 7229 9084

No performance of any kind may be given unless a licence has
been obtained. Applications should be made before rehearsals
begin. Publication of this play does not necessarily indicate its
availability for amateur performance.